Deep down we know that all is on loan to us. Accidents happen, disease spreads, storms come, aging continues, jobs terminate, mistakes occur. We go to bed one evening feeling good about life and ourselves. We awake in the morning and during the course of that day our world can be turned upside down by news of the death of a loved one, or an unexpected rift in a friendship, or the loss of a priceless possession, or a doctor's prognosis, or an unexpected financial decision.

For the one who believes that all is on loan, this is to be expected. Not that this expectation cripples the spirit of joy. Just the opposite is true; the present moment is treasured and enjoyed all the more because it is so precious and so fleeting. . . .

PRAYING
OUR
GOODBYES

Joyce Rupp, OSM

IVY BOOKS • NEW YORK

Ivy Books
Published by The Random House Publishing Group
Copyright © 1988 by Ave Maria Press

Library of Congress Catalog Card Number: 87-72291

Ivy Books and colophon are trademarks of Random House, Inc.

www.ballantinebooks.com

ISBN 0-8041-1060-3

This edition published by arrangement with Ave Maria Press

First Ballantine Books Edition: October 1992

Cover photo by E. Nagele/FPG International

OPM 22 21 20 19 18 17 16 15 14

Dedication

To Dad
his wisdom, laughter,
enthusiasm for life
and deep love of the earth
are among my greatest treasures

and

to Emily Palmer, O.S.M.,
Servite sister and friend,
her courage in living
and in dying
has blessed me

Contents

Acknowledgments

As I completed each section of the manuscript, I sent copies for comment to a diverse group of people, each of whom has had specific experiences of goodbye. Their suggestions to improve the content and style of the manuscript were tremendously helpful. I offer deep gratitude to: Fred Brunk, M.D. medical oncologist, and his wife, Mary Brunk, Ph.D. clinical specialist in oncology, both at Penn Clinic in Des Moines, Iowa; Bernard and Joan McLauglin, a retired couple from Logan, Iowa; Rev. Tom Pfeffer, pastor of a rural parish in Iowa; Margaret Ann Schmidt, family counselor for Lutheran Social Services, and her husband, Art Schmidt, chaplain and director of the CPE program at St. Joseph's Hospital in Tacoma, Washington; and Joy Weideman, O.S.M., former provincial of the Servites and currently English/Literature teacher at Heelan High School in Sioux City, Iowa.

I grow ever more grateful for my editor at Ave Maria Press, Frank Cunningham; his keen insights and his challenges enabled me to bring my best to this book.

Judy Green's sense of humor, patience and great secretarial skills blessed every page of the manuscript.

Much of my writing was done in two places of beauty and solitude. My thanks to these gracious people and the hospitality with which they always greeted me: Sharon Samek and her son, Scott, for use of their Colorado mountain home, and the Benedictine sisters at Covenant Monastery in Harlan, Iowa.

All of the participants in my courses, workshops and retreats have helped to shape this book, along with others who critiqued the goodbye prayers out of their lived experiences, did research for me, or helped by consultation. In particular, I thank Janet Barnes, Rev. Glenda Dietrich, Jackie Donaldson, Sid Drumheller, Rosaria Edney, O.S.M., Joyce Hutchison, Dolores Klein, Carolyn McCann, Rev. Frank Nelson and his wife, Rosemary, and Macrina Wiederkehr, O.S.B.

The perceptions that I gained from my own goodbyes would never have been expressed without very skilled and caring spiritual directors in my life. Thanks to Sandy Vadun, I.H.M., Tom Lukaszewicz, S.J. and Shirley Waldschmitt, O.S.F., for their grace-full guidance during my significant bends in the road.

Finally, I express a special thank you to all those who kept encouraging me to continue to write and for all those who keep telling me that they are praying for me. I especially thank my wonderful mother, Hilda, and my brothers and sisters; I am also very grateful to my religious family, the women in my Servite community who stand by me and continually offer their affirmation and support. *Praying Our Goodbyes* carries the touch of many special people. I shall always be grateful for how they helped this book to become a reality.

Preface

It was 1968. I had never thought about anyone in my family dying. I was young and they all seemed so full of life. Then came the phone call and my sister's voice saying, "I am so sorry to have to be the one to tell you. We lost Dave today. . . ." My 23-year-old brother, the one next in age to me, had drowned. Dave was the one I dearly loved and had yearned to know better. The memory of our last time together flashed through my mind: Dave, sitting in the easy chair smiling at me, and I, feeling a kind of sadness because we had so much yet to learn and to share with one another. Our time together had seemed all too short. Strange how I remember the exact words and know precisely what I was doing at the moment when the phone rang. The shock of that message deeply embedded the details in my memory.

The painful truth of how hard it is to say goodbye started to root itself and take hold in my heart. As I look back, I feel as though I have had this book in my soul for a long, long time. While it is a book about farewell to our loved ones who have died, it is also about many other forms of goodbye in our lives, all those events and experiences in which we feel a deep sense of loss. I believe that instead of running from these goodbyes, we need to take the time to reflect upon them, to "pray them." In doing so we can become wiser, deeper and more compassionate.

Although life is difficult and always has its share of sorrows, life is also very good and deeply enriching. It holds many promises of growth and treasures of joy. It is not easy to believe this when we are hurting greatly because of our loss. Sometimes it takes years to understand and accept this truth. That is how it has been for me.

The grief of losing my brother touched numerous areas of my life. I found myself fighting, avoiding, struggling with and being angry or confused about the many forms of goodbye that I experienced: being uprooted from one place to another, deaths of family friends and a dear uncle, termination of a significant friendship of many years, betrayal by one I had really trusted, struggles with church changes and with religious life decisions. Always the inner question "Why me?" accompanied any deep hurt or demands to let go. I kept asking, "Why should I experience the hard things in life when I am trying my best to be good?" I also had an angry "Not me!" and a pitiable "Poor me!" that rose up inside my aching spirit. Over the years I developed an attitude that said life was always supposed to be a continuous hello. The hurt and wrenching ache of goodbye was not supposed to be there.

Eventually I accepted the fact that life is unfair at times, that it has its share of difficulties no matter how good I am or how much I am yearning for happiness. I began to realize that I could become a more whole human being because of the way that life sometimes pressed painfully against my happiness and my deep desire to have everything go well. I know that although

I will sometimes feel broken apart or empty, eventually I will mend and be filled again.

Loss will never be easy for me, but I am much better at identifying the need to let go and at understanding the call to move on as a means of growth. Sometimes goodbyes still overwhelm me, but my questions are changing. Instead of asking ''Why me?'' I much more readily ask ''How?''—How can I move gracefully through the ache of the farewells that come into my life? I also ask ''Who?''—Who will be with me in this process?—because I know that I cannot go through intense leave-takings without some kinship and some loving support to sustain me.

These new questions have grown in my consciousness because of a very graced moment several years ago. The reality of my battle with goodbyes finally asserted itself one early morning as I walked across the beautiful University of Notre Dame campus. I found myself on a green lawn, facing a Pieta. The Pieta was shocking to me, stark and harsh, so unlike the soft, curving, feminine touch of Michelangelo's Woman and Son. This Pieta had sharp, angular features. The figures were full of holes. It was a black, metallic affront to my eyes, speaking loudly of suffering, of pain and agony. I could hardly bear to look at it, and I wanted to run away. But something inside of me drew me to sit and keep my eyes focused on the Woman of Sorrows who held her dead Son in her arms. Strong, powerful emotions pushed tears to my eyes. I hated the unfairness of life. I resented it in every fiber of my being. But I felt a deep yearning to discover a truth I had never possessed. As I looked and looked at the depiction of sorrow, the pain of goodbye seared through my gaze. I saw there a tremendous union of love, great strength, coupled with a heart-wrenching moment of lamentation and agony at life's unfairness. Truly this Pieta spoke more deeply the harsh truth of farewell than anything I had ever seen.

Deep within me the words came: "You must face goodbyes. You must come to terms with life's unfairness. You cannot allow your 'poor me's' and 'not me's' to stunt your growth any longer. You need to use your energy to give life, not to fight death." I continued to sit there for a long time.

When I arose, I knew what I had to do. I would walk the path of Jesus in a 30-day Ignatian retreat, a retreat that takes one into the paschal mystery with its loss and sorrow, its hope and resurrection. I would stop running. I'd throw myself into God's arms and I would ask God all those questions that were forever rising up to choke me. I would spend my days with Jesus: What would he say about life's losses? What was the meaning of his own life and suffering?

That moment of decision was one of the greatest graces of my life. My 30 days with God and a wonderful retreat directress changed my inner focus. So many essential, life-giving wisdoms surfaced during those days: the hello-goodbye pattern as an integral part of all human existence, the necessity of change in order to have growth, and the need to let go before one can truly move on. I also learned that the cost of discipleship is inherent in any following of Jesus and that this following causes choices which mean goodbye to some parts of life and hello to others.

Most important, I discovered that for the Christian, hello always follows goodbye in some form if we allow it. There is, or can be, new life, although it will be different from the life we knew before. The resurrection of Jesus and the promises of God are too strong to have it be any other way.

Introduction

Goodbyes are as much a part of life as the seasons of the year. The story of gain and loss, of joy and sorrow, of life and death, of union and separation, is inside each one of us. The cycle begins at birth, when we were broken loose from our mother's womb. Our forward movement gathered momentum until we pushed farewell and, with a throbbing burst of new life, cried hello again to a vastly different world.

The cycle continues throughout our lives. Who of us has not said farewell to someone and felt a great heartache and a deep sadness, wanting to stop the process and wondering when the ache inside would ever leave? Several years ago I accompanied a friend to the bus depot. She had been away for three years and was leaving again for a long time. The moment of separation came, that last little space when an onrush of sadness suddenly wells up and causes a great inadequacy of expression. Margaret turned and hugged me. Then she looked at me with tears in her eyes and painfully remarked: "We've said goodbye so often. Do you think that we will ever learn how?"

The word *goodbye*—originally "God-be-with-ye" or "Go-with-God"—was a recognition that God was a significant part of the going. When you dreaded or feared the journey there was strength in remembering that the One who gave and cherished life would be there to protect and to console. Goodbye was a blessing of love, proclaiming the belief that if God went with you, you would never be alone, that comfort, strength and all the other blessings of a loving presence would accompany you. To the traveler it meant: "We cannot keep you from this journey. We hurt deeply . . . you have made your home in our hearts. Yet, we know your leaving is essential for your growth. So go, go with God. May you always rest in the assurance that 'God will lead you, will be with you, will not fail you or desert you. Have no fear. Do not be disheartened by anything' (Dt 31:8)."

Do we ever get used to saying goodbye? Or should we? I think not. Saying goodbye helps us to experience the depths of our human condition. It leads us to a much deeper understanding of what it means to live life in its mystery and its wholeness. We ought not to be afraid of the partings that life asks of us. Nor ought we to hold back in giving ourselves fully to love, to the wonderful growth opportunities of investing ourselves in people and events.

We may be harshly bruised by life's farewells, but it is possible to be healed. We can become whole again. I believe that if we are willing to move inside the heart of the experience, to live patiently through the process even as we acknowledge the difficult, painful emotions, that we can experience the wonder of spiritual growth and the marvel of new depths of faith in our relationship with God and with others.

I teach a course titled "Praying Our Goodbyes." My goal is to have participants approach their leave-takings from a faith-dimension, knowing full well how important the psychological is as a foundation. This approach means a move from *saying* a goodbye to *praying* a goodbye. Each time that I present the material on this subject and listen to men's and women's responses and reflections, I re-learn that leave-takings are a part of everyone's life and that the human spirit is wonderfully resilient in recovering from them.

I learn so much from the participants in my classes. A woman dying of cancer reminded me by her presence not to be glib about the process of death; a recently divorced man who cried out one evening, "But what does 'letting go' mean?" helped me to approach that topic with more sensitivity and care. A young widow who could not forgive God for her husband's death cautioned me not to be too naive in my assumptions when speaking about the strength we can receive from our faith as we are struggling with our losses.

As I continued to develop the material for future classes, I began to see an important network of premises and concepts that needed to be included if one was going to pray a goodbye or come through a farewell with spiritual health and growth. These premises and concepts are the content of the chapters of this book.

I have discovered many women and men seeking help for their prayer life in moments of goodbye, times when they feel incapable of praying in the way that they once knew or in the way that once seemed so right for them. Prayers which use ritual and symbol are comforting and healing ways to express and reflect upon pain and hurt. The prayers found in the final section of this book are for this purpose. They can be used in a variety of ways for a great many kinds of farewells.

There are questions at the end of each chapter which can be used by individuals or for group sharing.

It is my hope that the readers of *Praying Our Goodbyes* will see that hurts, pains and losses need not destroy them but rather can lead to a better understanding of life, a greater wisdom and compassion, and a deeper

courage to continue the journey that will eventually take
us all home. Goodbyes will always be with us. So will
hellos. Praying a goodbye can bring us to the doorway
of new beginnings. The seed of resurrection in our souls
will grow again.

CHAPTER ONE

✧

The Ache of Autumn in Us

> There is a season for everything,
> a time for giving birth,
> a time for dying;
> a time for tears,
> a time for laughter;
> a time for mourning,
> a time for dancing. . . .
>
> —Ecclesiastes 3:1,2,4

The trees grow more restless;
October wind weaves through them;
they shake their arms in dismay
as if to fight the coming cold
and the grief of leaves going.

Autumn air does a heart-dance
on branches already gone barren;
the misty air clings to golden leaves,
making the trees bend even lower.

It is a season to hold the trees close,
to stand with them in their grieving.
It is a time to open my inner being
to the misty truths of my own goodbyes.

Autumn comes. It always does.
Goodbye comes. It always does.
The trees struggle with this truth today
and in my deepest of being, so do I.

Every autumn, nostalgia fills me;
every autumn, yearning holds me.

I cling to the ripeness of summer,
knowing it will be many long months
before I can catch a breath of lilac,
or the green of freshly mown grass.

And so I begin my fallow vigil,
remembering the truth of the ages:
Unless the wheat seed dies
it cannot sing a new birth.
Unless summer gives in to autumn
springtime will never embrace me.

Every autumn reminds me of my vulnerability. It carries the truth that life is fragile, that there are no sure guarantees for a trouble-free life, that there is always some dying in living, that change is inevitable. I was reminded of this in a particularly harsh way last October. There was a beautiful young linden tree just outside my office window. It was a golden glory in the sunshine, full of bright yellow, autumn leaves. One morning a strong wind came from the grey northeast sky. I stood and watched that young tree as every last leaf was stripped and torn away. In less than an hour the tree stood in nakedness, a golden circle of summer's growth at its feet.

I hurt for the tree in its emptiness. Then slowly I saw myself as the linden, moving through my own life stages, knowing how I, too, have sometimes felt the harsh blows of a ripping away. I stood by the window of my inner world and saw the story of transformation pass before me in invitation. At that moment I prayed hard and deep for openness and for the gift not to fight the process of goodbye.

But as I looked at the empty tree, my prayer became barely a whisper. All those beautiful leaves on the ground, the seemingly tragic stripping of a tree full of life! I felt that no part of me could easily say yes to an experience like that. As I turned away from the window I sensed a kinship with autumn. It had spoken loudly about the way life is with its going, grieving, growing story.

There is an "ache" in autumn that is also within each one of us. This ache is the deep stillness of a late September morning when mist covers the land and the sound of geese going south fills the sky. There is a wordless yearning or a longing for something in the air, and it penetrates the human spirit. It is a tender, nostalgic desire to gather our treasures and hold them close because the ache tells us that someday those treasures will need to be left behind. Autumn speaks to this pain in our own spirits, that ache which we try so hard to ignore or deny or push aside, that little persistent reminder that death is always a part of life.

The ache of autumn that is in us has two faces: One is an ache that lies deep down inside our being. The other is the ache that results from our own individual, particular losses—those farewells that are always going on in our lives.

The Existential Ache

One author speaks of an "existential loneliness" that permeates every human spirit, a kind of unnamed pain inside, deep within us, a restlessness, an anxiety, a sense of "all aloneness" that calls out to us. I prefer to name it an "existential ache." It is a persistent longing in us and it happens because we are human. It is as strongly present in us as autumn is present in the cycle of the seasons. I believe that this ache is within us because we are composed of both physical and spiritual dimensions. Our body belongs to the earth but our spirit does not. Our final home is not here, although "here" is where we are meant to be transformed by treasuring, reverencing and growing through our human journey. No matter how good the "good earth" is, there is always a part of us that is yearning, longing, quietly crying out for the true homeland where life is no longer difficult or unfair.

Every once in a while we get in touch with this truth in us. It is not a sadness exactly, not a hurt or a pain as such, but some tremendously deep voice that cries out in bitter-sweet agony. We catch a glimpse of home and the possibility of who we are meant to be, and this entices us hopefully. But at the same time, we also catch a glimpse of how far we have yet to go; we see that there are many twists and bends and struggles in the road before we arrive home, and this glimpse pains us with its reality. It is the autumn in all of us, the truth that life can never stay just as it is.

This inner ache is felt especially when we sense the mystery of life or the supreme uniqueness of who we are. It is present when we recognize the fleetingness of all that we know and all that we cling to upon this good earth. We have a strong longing at this moment to hold onto all of it and we realize the impossibility of doing so. We seldom put words on this melancholy. We only dimly sense its presence. But it colors our moods and pervades our activities and weaves its way through our unconscious. It is present in our edginess or in blue days that seem to have no cause. It raises its voice in our inability to concentrate or to feel full satisfaction, even when everything in our lives is going smoothly. It makes itself felt when, perhaps just for a brief moment, we recognize our mortality and the swiftness with which time passes.

There will always be a corner of our heart where it is autumn, that part of us which aches with searching and loneliness, with restlessness or dissatisfaction. It is Augustine's "Our hearts are made for you, O Lord, and they will not rest until they rest in you." It will remain in us until we are truly home.

What about those who never seem to have this experience? Some never recognize the ache for what it is, while others push away these feelings and awarenesses as far from themselves as possible. They cannot bear the message. The ache is not comfortable and some ignore it or run away from it by being so busy that they do not have time to think or feel anything too deeply. Some press harder in their work; some rush out to buy things when they feel lonely or down. Some always seek out others so they will not have to listen to that sense of incompleteness within themselves. Radios and televisions that are always on may be attempts to block out the truth that lies within.

Not that we should be self-absorbed by our inner ache, but it is very worthwhile to acknowledge it. This loneliness, paradoxically, joins us with all others in their aloneness. There is a great strength and comfort in this. It is only when we are willing to meet the absolute truth of that aloneness within us that we are no longer alone, that we are able to break through to a level of consciousness that assures us of the magnificent bonding that we have with other humans and with God. We begin to see the ache as a natural part of our humanity and of our inner journey. This awareness and bonding can be a source of a deep and rich spiritual growth. We realize that we are not the only ones who are going home, that we are not the only ones who are still un-

finished, that we are not the only ones whose lives call
us to many partings before we are at one with the eternal hello. Kenneth Leech expresses it this way:

> True self-love means not trying to escape from our-
> selves, but listening to the voices within us. . . . This
> involves the acceptance of our fundamental alone-
> ness, not seeking to reduce it, not hoping that
> friendship, marriage, community, or group, will take
> it away. That aloneness is an integral part of being
> human, and an essential element in love. It is out of
> that aloneness that it becomes possible to respond
> rather than merely react to people and needs. Re-
> sponse has to grow and emerge out of the depths of
> myself: it is *my* response, born out of my inner
> struggle and inner self-knowledge, out of my spirit,
> my deepest core. This is what spirituality is about.[1]

If we are attentive to the inner ache, and if we grow
in accepting its truthful message, then we will more
readily move through our own particular goodbyes. We
will be more open to the growth of the human journey.

The Ache of Particular Goodbyes

Goodbyes are a part of every single day. Sometimes
we choose them, and sometimes they choose us. Usually they are small, not so significant losses that do not
pain us very much, but at times they are deep, powerful, wounding experiences that trail around our hearts
and pain inside of us for years.

What is a goodbye? It is an empty place in us. It is
any situation in which there is some kind of loss, some

1. Kenneth Leech, *True Prayer*: An Introduction to Christian Spirituality (London: Sheldon Press, 1980), p. 44.

incompleteness, when a space is created in us that cries out to be filled. Goodbyes are any of those times when we find ourselves without a someone or a something that has given our life meaning and value, when a dimension of our life seems to be out of place or unfulfilled. Goodbyes are all of those experiences that leave us with a hollow feeling someplace deep inside.

We say goodbye to parents, spouses, children, friends, sometimes just for a day or a year, and sometimes until we meet them on the other side of this life. We leave familiar places and secure homes. We bid farewell to strong, healthy bodies, burdenfree spirits or minds. We change teachers, schools, parishes and managers, sometimes spouses or religion. We change our ideas, our values, our self-image and our way of interpreting life's situations. We place parents in nursing care homes, allow children to experience risk-taking and growth, say no to love relationships that would be inappropriate or possibly harmful to us or to others. All these hard decisions and choices that we make or experience involve some kind of leave-taking.

In our work world we experience transfers, changes in skills, different positions and retirement; in natural disasters such as fires, floods, storms of all kinds we lose significant material possessions that can never be reclaimed. Illness, whether our own or of loved ones, demands a farewell to some of our independence or to our mobility and strength, to our energy and, perhaps, to our sexual drive. We say goodbye through our aging process. We bid adieu to a part of ourselves and others as children grow up and grow away, as we experience relationship adjustments on all levels. There are goodbyes in our ongoing conversion of heart when we let go of non-truths, of sinful, worn ways or old angers or antipathies that have consumed us. We also experience farewells in adult transitions where we struggle with self-image, goals and dreams. It may be a time of letting go of our hope of being the best, or of having the perfect parents or the perfect family or the perfect community. These goodbyes that seem to last forever reflect the inner ache of autumn with its hollowness and emptiness.

Identifying our Goodbyes

When the goodbyes are big ones such as the death of a loved one or a divorce, we have no trouble recognizing them. It is the lesser goodbyes that we can avoid or not acknowledge and, in doing so, miss the inner direction and the value of growth they offer us. The following questions may be of help in identifying those goodbyes.

1) *What hurts you now?*
   What distresses you, worries you, causes you negative feelings such as anger, envy, jealousy, self-pity, discouragement, anxiety, fear? Is there any part of your life that feels lost?

2) *What do you wish you could get rid of in your life?*
   Is it a deep sense of loss due to the death of a loved one, your own illness or a physical pain, a problem at work or at home, a great loneliness, a sinfulness, the hurried pace of life, some guilt, irritating persons, your own lack of mental or spiritual or social growth, another's illness, your own aging, an old memory, an enemy? What would you like to never have to experience again?

3) *What do you wish that you could have more of in your life?*
   Would it be faith, friendships, personal giftedness

and talents, money, hope, sense of direction, security, good health, a feeling of being that special someone in another's life, time to be with those you love, companionship, freedom, truth? What is it that you most yearn for?

4) *How does it hurt you?*

Is your response one of self-preoccupation or self-centeredness, bodily distress, poor self-image or lack of belief in self, depression, distrust, keeping others shut out, anxiety attacks, misdirected anger, loneliness, emptiness, loss of security, lack of concentration, feelings of failure? How are you (or how is your life) different because of this hurt?

Once we recognize and come to terms with how a goodbye is hurting us, we can begin the process of working with it. For example, if we are letting our pain take us too far from others and too much into self-centeredness, we can begin taking steps to get more involved in the lives of others. If our goodbye is affecting our lack of peace by its anger or bitterness, we can begin to acknowledge those feelings, expressing them in a healthy way and gradually be freed of them. Only after we have acknowledged our losses and have recognized the pain inherent in these goodbyes can we proceed on the journey of self-growth and greater love of others.

The Value of Goodbyes

Goodbyes, especially the more intense ones, cause us to face the ultimate questions of life: Why suffering?

Where am I headed? What are my most cherished values? What do I believe about life after death? Goodbyes create a certain space in us where we allow ourselves room to look at life in perspective and to gradually discover answers to some of those questions about life. We also learn a lot about the significant others in our lives; we learn who is willing to walk the long road with us, whose heart always welcomes us no matter what, who loves us enough to stand with us in good times and in bad, who is willing to love us enough to speak the truth for us or to us. Goodbyes, when reflected upon in faith, can draw us to a greater reliance upon the God of love, our most significant other. With God we can learn to live in hope, with greater meaning and deeper joy. All this only comes with time and with great care of self.

We cannot avoid the ache of autumn. We all hurt in our own way but we do hurt. The blessedness in the ache within us is that when we grieve over the farewells, we both give ourselves and find ourselves. We become one with whoever and whatever has met us on our journey. We choose to invest ourselves deeply even though we know that the investment might cost us the price of goodbyes and letting go. We believe that the investment of our love is worth it, for we have entered into the mystery of life where the hellos that follow our goodbyes are our guideposts to the eternal home.

We all need to learn how to say goodbye, to acknowledge the pain that is there for us so that we can eventually move on to another hello. When we learn how to say goodbye we truly learn how to say to ourselves and to others: ''Go, God be with you. I entrust you to God. The God of strength, courage, comfort, hope, love, is with you. The God who promises to wipe away all tears will hold you close and will fill your emptiness. Let go and be free to move on. Do not keep yourself from another step in your homeward journey. May the blessing of the God of autumn be with you."

Questions for Reflection, Integration, Discussion:

1. People experience many kinds of goodbyes. Which do you think is the most difficult?

2. Write down the word *autumn*. Next to it (or under it) write words and phrases that come to your mind as you think of autumn. What is your predominant feeling about autumn?

3. What are the goodbyes that are currently happening in your life? Which is the hardest for you? What makes it so difficult?

4. What is the goodbye through which you have experienced the most growth? What made it so for you?

5. What do you see as the greatest value in your goodbyes?

CHAPTER TWO

✧

I Know How the Flowers Felt

> The rain to the wind said,
> "You push and I'll pelt."
> They so smote the garden bed
> That the flowers actually knelt,
> And lay lodged—though not dead
> I know how the flowers felt.[1]
>
> —Robert Frost

If you have ever said a deeply significant goodbye, you know "how the flowers felt," you know what it is like to have life pelt you with sorrow, to be overwhelmed with emptiness, loneliness, confusion and sadness. At these times we are bent over, crushed, like the flowers that "lay lodged—though not dead." The pain is overwhelming, often too deep for tears. The sorrow of it can pervade one's whole self and hurt in every part of one's being. No medicine, no bandage, no diversion, no luxury, no words can assuage the hurt and give it the freedom to desist and cease its painful bending, almost breaking, of the heart. Time and the strength of God's presence can lessen the pain, but even these gifts cannot take the pain away or cure it completely. Just when we think that the last bit of goodbye is out of our heart, we hear someone's name, or we recall a memory, or we have another dream, or we see a house that looks like the one we left, or an old wound

1. "The Poems of Robert Frost," *The Modern Library* (New York: Henry Holt and Co., 1946), p. 273.

of the spirit flares up in our consciousness, and the pain is suddenly very real again.

Every goodbye has some suffering in it and the greater the parting the deeper the pain; the greater the loss, the more severe is the empty place that accompanies it. Some of us feel the hurt more than others. So much depends on our personality, our personal history, our God relationship, and our own philosophy of life. People who are deep feeling will usually ache over goodbyes a great deal more than those who approach life on a more intellectual, analytical level. People whose families brush the hurt of loss aside or cover it up with silence, busyness or other ways of avoidance will probably find themselves doing the same thing, not realizing how intense the loss actually is. No matter how we stuff it away or avoid it, however, the pain of goodbyes will show itself in our lives at some time.

I listen to the story of one who has lost a dearly beloved spouse and I wonder if there can be any goodbye so deep as that death in a person's life. I hear the agony of one who has recently been divorced, who has experienced the death of love itself. "Surely," I say to myself, "this goodbye is one of the deepest wounds of all." Then a young man comes into my life, talented and promising, and he suffers a broken neck in a swimming accident, paralyzed for life, forced to say goodbye to many of his dreams for the future. I realize how intense his inner pain is. I meet a man who has been in deep depression because of a forced early retirement. He tells me with tears in his eyes how his whole identity has been that of his work world. He has spent a year struggling with questions about the value of his life and its purpose. It has been a year full of suffering.

The stories go on and on and so does the hurt inherent in them. No two people say goodbye in exactly the same way and no two people suffer their farewells in the same way, but suffer they do. That is why the mystery of suffering must be considered when one is reflecting on the losses in life.

The painful feelings that accompany any grieving process or time of loss are on all levels of our being: physical, emotional, mental or spiritual. When we grieve, we leave behind someone or something very precious to us. We can expect to have any or all of the following feelings: shock, sadness, depression, denial. There may be volatile emotions of hostility or intense yearnings, tearfulness, restlessness, fears and anxieties of all kinds. We may feel that there is no one who can understand our grief. We may not be able to concentrate on our work or our responsibilities and we may even think that we are losing our minds because we feel so disoriented and fragmented inside. We will probably be angry and feel guilty over something unsaid or undone. We might have resentment and self-pity for a time. There is often a sense of being lost. We may feel that no one cares, not even God who has always been there for us. There may also be a pain in our body where there was never pain before: headaches, backaches, stomach aches or other symptoms. During our darkest and loneliest of times, we are sometimes frightened by our loss of enthusiasm, our thoughts of "Why go on?" or of "Why even bother to get out of bed today?" We often feel drained of the desire to do anything that requires our investment and our energy. It is hard to go on believing and trying to live during times of great loss.[2]

2. Granger E. Westberg, *Good Grief* (Philadelphia: Fortress Press, 1962, 1972). Chapters one through ten identify and explore many of the emotions associated with grief.

The suffering and the sensation of hurting deep within our personal system gradually diminishes with time. At the moment we are experiencing the anguish of the goodbye, however, it seems as though it will never go away. We feel like the flowers, crushed and over-whelmed by the inner storm.

These painful feelings come in varying degrees with the many forms of goodbye that are a part of life. They also come when we deliberately make certain choices. We say farewell to other options when we accept the decisions we have made. Suffering is especially sharp when the choices are between options that both look beneficial: Do I go on that trip with my spouse who so much needs my presence now in his mid-life struggle, or do I stay home with our children who are at such a crucial adolescent age? Do I continue with chemother-apy which makes me so ill but prolongs my life, or do I discontinue it and enjoy the quality of life I now have? Do I place my mother in a nursing home where health care is so much better, or do I continue to support her in the situation of living alone where she feels so much more secure and at peace but is also much more prone to accidents? Do I file for divorce because it is so ob-vious that my marriage has died and is death-dealing to both my spouse and to myself, or do I go on choosing to remain in the situation because the children need the two of us to be there for them? Oftentimes it is very hard to live peacefully with the choices that one has to make.

Life is Unfair

Much of how we learn to live and grow through the suffering of our goodbyes has to do with how we look at the cause of that suffering. When people are in the middle of hard moments, when they are trying to account for "life accidents" (those unplanned for, unpredictable parts of life), they often try to find someone or something to explain their cause.[3] People who are suffering often conclude that life is unfair. But what they may actually mean is: Why isn't God fair? The expectation is that good should come to the good and bad to the bad. If we have been good we should not have the hard, ugly blows of life. Isn't that how God ought to operate? Why isn't God fair? Isn't God the one who is ultimately to blame for this pain? Couldn't this God, who can do all things, have stopped it in an instant?

How often this attitude toward suffering is voiced by those who have been hurt because of goodbyes. Parents who have taken so much time with their children and have done their best to share good values with them are wounded by their children's choices of lifestyles and substance abuse. Their inner voices are a mixture of guilt and anger at life's unfairness: "Where did we go wrong? Why has life dealt us this humiliating blow? Why has God let this happen?" The woman who battles depression all her life wonders the same thing. Something in her keeps pulling at her self-esteem and dragging away her joy as she goes on saying goodbye to her inner energy and enthusiasm. She looks at others who have never had this long, emotional war and she wonders: "Why me? What have I done? What more could I do? Why hasn't God taken this away?" A man who deeply loves his wife and struggles hard to make life good for her and their five children is left in loneliness after her death in a car accident. He cries out in anger

3. Gail Sheehy, *Pathfinders* (New York: Bantam Books, 1981), pp. 383–428.

and agony: "Why my wife? Why me? Why us? Why didn't you prevent the accident, God?" Or the woman who wakes up one day to discover that the husband she has felt so close to has chosen a new life with one of his employees. She is wracked with the pain of betrayal and personal rejection and she, too, cries out that she has been given something that she doesn't deserve. The farmer who has worked and worked to hold onto his land is given the devastating decision of foreclosure by his bank. Market prices, drought and storms were too much for him. He walks across his land for one last time saying goodbye to a way of life that has meant so much, and he wonders what he did wrong that life could treat him so cruelly. All of these people have come face to face with a reality of the human condition: Life *is* unfair. Life does not always treat us kindly. They have also come face to face with the deep questions of good-byes: What does God have to do with my suffering? Why does life have to be this way?

False Theories About Suffering

A woman recently shared with me how she had tried to account for the pain in her life. She had suffered from osteoporosis for a major portion of her life and was always hurting, in and out of the hospital with broken bones. One evening she had an opportunity to go to a faith-healing service. She said to the faith-healer, "I don't know what I'm doing here; I think God wants me to have this suffering for a reason." The healer replied, "God doesn't want you to have this. God wants you to be whole, happy in body, mind and spirit." She looked at him in surprise and said, "Well, if God didn't send this to me, who *can* I blame?"

Who can we blame? If we listen closely to those who hurt or those who are trying to console someone who hurts, we can hear in their remarks a certain belief about who causes suffering and why. Their beliefs usually center around one of the following reasons: First, God sends the hurt, the bitter loss, because he loves us so much. Thus, the greater our difficulties, the greater is God's love for us because suffering is a purification and a means of transformation. (A sister in my community who had numerous operations for malignant growths was once told: "You must be loved very specially by God to have been given all of this suffering." She replied, "Well, then, I wish God didn't love me so much!") Another belief says that God sends pain because we are being punished for some sin of the past. There is guilt in this belief and oftentimes added sorrow because of the feeling that the sufferers indirectly caused God to send the suffering. They believe it would not have happened had it not been for their sin. (A young couple were deeply grieved at the death of their two-year-old son. When he died they concluded that God had taken their child because he was born out of wedlock.) Thirdly, some think that God sends the suffering to test them, to see if they really have faith and to prove their love for God in times of trial. Finally, there is a belief that God sends suffering for some reason that we do not understand. People often say, "It is God's will for us and we must simply accept it if we are to be good and faithful followers."

Not one of these four beliefs is an accurate approach for understanding the suffering of our broken places or for living through them. The major premise in all of these beliefs is false. *God does not send suffering to us.* We still have a lot of unhealthy thinking in our theology of suffering. Whenever we say "God sends suffering" we are entering into pagan-tinged territory. In ancient times people also struggled with the ache and pain that came into their human existence. They questioned the elements: Why lightning and storms that destroyed? Why no rain or why too much sun for the crops? Why infertility for some women and not for others? Why death, disease or other calamities that crippled and stole life? They began to see all these mysterious struggles as coming from some hidden power in the situation. Something or someone was sending them good or bad things. They developed a theory that if they appeased the mysterious powers, which they presumed caused good or bad to happen, then they would be spared life's travails and pains. The gods, as these powers were later named, would then be good to them in return and would not send them suffering.

This theology of suffering, based on an appeasement of the gods who had power over them, was carried over into Old Testament stories. Recall the story of Abraham who was asked to kill his only son on the altar of sacrifice to prove his faith in the true God (Gn 22). A messenger of God entered in and stopped Abraham. When this happened a tradition of thought was broken: no more human sacrifices to appease the one true God. It was a breakthrough, but the idea of sacrifices of appeasement persisted for a long, long time as we can see in the New Testament approach that refers to Jesus as being a scapegoat or an appeasement sacrifice to the Father (1 Cor 6:20; 1 Pt 1:19; Heb 10:1-18).

The testing approach to suffering has also been held for many years. In the story of Job the author tells us that God tested Job by destroying everyone that Job loved and everything of value that Job owned. What kind of God would do this? The author of the Book of

Job was struggling with the mystery of suffering just as we do and concluded that God was a testing God.

The thought that God sends suffering as a punishment for our sins is expressed throughout humanity's history, throughout the Old Testament and in the New Testament. When Jesus is with the disciples they ask him about a blind man: "Rabbi, who sinned, this man or his parents, for him to have been born blind?" Jesus answered them, "Neither he nor his parents sinned. He was born blind so that the works of God might be displayed in him" (Jn 9:2-3). At another time Jesus himself raised the same kind of question in order to dispel the theory of suffering as a punishment for sin. When "some people arrived and told him about the Galileans whose blood Pilate had mingled with that of their sacrifices," Jesus said to them, "Do you suppose these Galileans who suffered like that were greater sinners than any other Galileans? They were not, I tell you" (Lk 13:1-3). In both cases Jesus is refuting the long held belief that the suffering of the man born blind, or of the murdered Galileans or of anyone in a similar position, is a punishment for sin. In each of these circumstances Jesus goes on to point out the necessity of repenting of one's sinfulness and suggests that instances such as these can be invitations for a change of heart or for inner conversion. In doing this, he implies that suffering *can* be an opportunity for us to reflect on our life, the kind of persons we are, how we relate to others, what we value, but Jesus flatly refuses to uphold the traditional theory that suffering is sent as a punishment for one's sins.

What about the will of God? Does God will our suffering? God does not send our suffering or want us to have it, but God does allow it to be there. Jesus himself struggled with the "will of the Father" when he was in his moment of agony (Lk 22:39-46). Jesus was fully human. He did not want the pain. He begged his Father to enter into his goodbye moment and to take away the pain: "Father," he said, "if you are willing, take this cup away from me." When Jesus continued with "Nevertheless, let your will be done, not mine," he was accepting his painful situation. The Father did not enter in, did not perform a miracle and keep him from the cross; he did not save Jesus from being human. He allowed Jesus to have full participation in the human condition just as all of us have to enter fully into it. God's will for us is that of our happiness, our peace of mind and heart. God does not will us or want us to suffer life's hurts, but God does allow the suffering to happen because, as Rabbi Kushner says so clearly, for God to do otherwise would be to block our human nature and our human condition.[4] Accidents do happen, death does come to us all, disease is prevalent in our world, but God is not *doing* those things to us. We are full and finite human beings living on an earth where natural disasters occur, where genetic conditions exist, where we sometimes make poor or sinful choices, where life does not always work as we had planned and hoped it would. We are blessed and burdened with our humanity, with the mystery of growing into a wholeness of personhood which involves continual goodbyes. We are frail and unfinished, subject always to the possibility of pain. We live in a world where we know we cannot escape our own mortality, our final goodbye before the eternal hello.

4. Harold S. Kushner, *When Bad Things Happen to Good People* (New York: Avon Books, 1981). See chapter three, "God Leaves Us Room to Be Human," pp. 72-86.

A God Who Cares

When we experience our goodbyes, we come face to face with questions about suffering. We also come face to face with a God who suffers pain and hurts with us, a God who wants us to be free of our suffering. Jesus gave evidence of this in his life by blessing and healing, freeing and consoling, doing all he could to take away the suffering that was part of the human condition. God is one who has promised over and over in the scriptures to be near with comfort for us, to be there to sustain us, to keep us from being destroyed by our difficulties (2 Cor 4:7-18; Rom 8:35-39; Is 43:1-5). This God is a refuge for the needy in distress, a shelter from the storm, a shade from the heat (Is 25:4), the good friend who stays with us in our struggles and our emptiness. I think of this God as being revealed in the woman in my community who comforted me when I received the phone call telling of my young brother's death. She came up and put her arm around my shoulders and held me as I cried. What a wonderful comfort I felt at that moment. I was not alone in my pain; I knew she cared; I knew she was there feeling the pain with me.

This God who stays with us in our struggles is the one described to me in a letter from a friend. She wrote:

> There is some resistance in me when dealing with my own pain and grief and relating it to God. I have had two experiences of God being with me in my suffering of the past three years. Part of me felt so abandoned that I didn't want any part of hearing about God. The other part of me knew of God's care, love and concern for me through the care, love and concern of those around me. It was in that that

I began discovering the responsibility I carried for my own life—and that God wasn't going to change events for me but would help me grow through them.

This compassionate, caring God is "like a shepherd feeding his flock, gathering the lambs in his arms, holding them against his breast" (Is 40:11). Isaiah tells us that we are so close to God that we are carved on the palm of God's hand, and that we will never be forgotten by God (Is 49:14-16). This is the God who consoles us when we feel our brokenness:

> *"Do not be afraid, for I have redeemed you;*
> *I have called you by your name, you are mine.*
> *Should you pass through the sea, I will be there*
> *   with you;*
> *or through rivers, they will not swallow you up.*
> *Should you walk through fire, you will not be*
> *scorched*
> *and the flames will not burn you. . . .*
> *You are precious in my eyes . . . I love you. . . .*
> *Do not be afraid, for I am with you"* (Is 43:2,4).

God's love is such a powerful companion for us that no matter how searing or how intense the hurt of a loss is we know that our spirit need not be destroyed by it; we know that God will help us to recover our hope, our courage and our direction in life.

If we allow ourselves to know God in this way, then we will have a very different approach to the will of God. As the authors of *Compassion* tell us:

God's will is not a label that can be put on unhappy situations. . . . Instead of declaring anything and everything to be the will of God, we must be willing to ask ourselves where in the midst of our pains and sufferings we can discern this loving presence of God.[5]

This loving presence of God can be our stronghold in our goodbyes. Our image of God is so important when we come to terms with suffering. If God is a God "out there" who is always demanding hard things for us in order to purify us or punish us, or if God is seen as always sending us sorrows in order to test us or challenge us to do some divine "will," or if God is seen as piling on suffering in order to show how much we are loved, then we will draw little comfort and consolation from our relationship with God during our goodbye times. We may, in fact, feel a lot of anger, bitterness, guilt and resentment toward this God.

Our awareness of the loving presence of God does not mean that we will never have moments of feeling angry at God or abandoned by God or be just plain unfeeling toward God during times of loss. These are natural, human responses of grief and some feel them more strongly than others. But we will not go on forever blaming God for causing the situation or for not intervening and stopping the event. If our image of God is a positive one, we will eventually return to a time when we recognize the comfort and love that are waiting there for us.

Our God is a God who dwells within, a loving presence near to us who yearns for our happiness, one who walks with us in our struggles. If our God is a God who holds us close "as a mother hen gathers her chicks" close to her (Mt 23:37), then we will come through our goodbyes with a deeper sense of being tenderly cared

5. Donald P. McNeill, Douglas A. Morrison, Henri J.M. Nouwen, *Compassion* (Garden City, N.Y.: Doubleday & Co., Inc., 1982), p. 40.

for by our God and we will draw comfort and strength from this presence. As Kushner writes:

> We can't pray that God will make our lives free of problems; this won't happen, and it is probably just as well. . . . But people who pray for courage, for strength to bear the unbearable, for the grace to remember what they have left instead of what they have lost, very often find their prayers answered. They discover that they have more strength, more courage than they ever knew themselves to have. Where did they get it? I would like to think that their prayers helped them find that strength. Their prayers helped them tap reserves of faith and courage which were not available to them before.[6]

Our One-Liners

Besides our understanding of the relationship between God and life's unfairness, there is another very vital element in our ability to grow through a goodbye moment. I call this element our "one-liners," those sayings we have inside of us which sum up our vision or philosophy of life. One day a woman in her early 30s came to see me, obviously distraught, confused and searching for peace in her life. She was single, had recently been betrayed by a man whom she thought really loved her, was feeling very overwhelmed by her work and was questioning where her relationship with God was in all of that. I remember so clearly how she looked at me with tears in her eyes and said with a sad smile of recognition: "I guess that I need some new one-liners in my life." She meant, of course, that she needed to re-evaluate her goals, those beliefs and phi-

6. Kushner, p. 125.

losophies that gave her inner direction, and to find a line that would tie all those together and give her a hopeful new thrust in life.

Our one-liners tell us a lot about what gets us through the tough times. Some one-liners that people have shared with me are:

This, too, will pass.

One day at a time.

In the end, it will all be okay.

God will provide.

Expect the unexpected.

No pain—no gain.

Make the most of each day.

Be good to yourself.

Life is a gift, never to be taken for granted.

Everyone needs to have another chance.

Even a perfect egg must break for new life to begin.

Life is what we make it.

Sometimes these one-liners wear thin or no longer have the power they once had for us and we need to find new ones because we have changed and have grown.

Nietzche said, "The one who has a *why* to live can bear with almost any *how*." Our philosophy of life often comes from wise persons we have known personally or through history. Viktor Frankl's vision of life has most influenced my own one-liners and has greatly enabled me to see that suffering can be a means of growth in wisdom and strength. Frankl was a psychotherapist who experienced the concentration camps. He was prisoner No. 119,104 at Auschwitz. There Frankl was stripped naked in his existence; everyone and everything he cherished was taken from him. In spite of his intense aloneness and loneliness, in spite of the horror of non-human conditions, Viktor Frankl not only survived the camp but developed a deep understanding of the human spirit. He searched to find meaning in life through his sufferings and he believed that if there was a purpose in life at all, there must be a purpose in suffering and dying. He firmly believed that our attitude toward suffering made all the difference in how we live our lives. In *Man's Search for Meaning* he says:

> When a man finds that it is his destiny to suffer, he will have to accept that suffering as his task; the single unique task. He will have to acknowledge the fact that even in suffering he is unique and alone in the universe. No one can relieve him of the suffering or suffer in his place. His unique opportunity lies in the way in which he bears his burden.[7]

The way that Viktor Frankl bore his burdens helped him to grow through the many goodbyes to loved ones, and to human dignity and freedom during his time at Auschwitz. The way that we bear our burdens can do

7. Viktor E. Frankl, *Man's Search for Meaning* (New York: Pocket Book Press, 1963, 1977), pp. 123–124.

the same. We have a choice in our theology of suffering and we have a choice in our response to the suffering that comes our way. We can respond with anger and bitterness by being stoical and not allowing ourselves to cry or to have anyone comfort us. We can be the martyr, full of self-pity, bemoaning our pain forever and becoming totally self-centered. We can give up, let ourselves stay depressed, stop trying to put life into our life, or we can gradually grow wiser and find deeper meaning in our existence.

We will probably experience many negative responses and feelings in our grieving (it is natural to do so), but if our vision of life is whole and hopeful, our goodbye pain will eventually lead us to compassion and to a deeper bonding with others who know hurt and sorrow. We will find ourselves readily and warmly embracing others who grieve because we have been down that long, lonely road of goodbyes and we know how blessed it is to have the touch of care beside us. We will not only know ''how the flowers felt,'' we will also know the powerful strength of a God who goes with us on that goodbye journey when we are bent over from the storms of life. It is this loving God who will enable our empty places to become sources of transformation, inner wisdom, compassion and tenderness.

Questions for Reflection, Integration, Discussion:

1. All goodbyes bring with them some kind of hurt and pain. What words would you use to describe the inherent suffering?

2. How do *you* explain life's unfairness?

3. We have wise persons in our lives who have given

us insights into suffering. Who is your wise person and what have you learned from him or her?

4. What is the one-liner that gets you through the suffering in your life?

5. What is your vision or philosophy of life? These questions will help you to put words on it:

Who/what is most important to you in your life?

What is most helpful for your personal growth?

How do you feel about change?

How do you usually respond to life's accidents?

What significance does God or religious faith have for you?

If you had only one year to live, how would you want to spend this time?

What do you want people to remember about you after you die?

CHAPTER THREE

✧

Hello—Goodbye—Hello

> A woman in childbirth suffers
> because her time has come;
> but when she has given birth to
>   the child she forgets the
>   suffering
> in her joy that (a child) has been
>   born into the world.
> So it is with you: you are sad now,
> but I shall see you again, and your
>   hearts will be full of joy,
> and that joy no one shall take from
>   you.
>
> —John 16:21-22

What does the life and message of Jesus tell us about the goodbyes in our lives? It tells us that he knew what it was like to go through those painful times. He, too, had many moments when he felt pulled apart, knew the hurt of leaving behind, felt the emptiness that comes with deep loss. Jesus was not spared the ache and the struggle of letting go. He knew the price of goodbyes. They had been with him all his life because he was so fully human, so much like all of us who travel the hello-goodbye-hello pattern of the human journey.

We do not know much about the years before his move out of Nazareth. We do know that "he grew in wisdom and stature . . ." (Lk 2:52). Because he was like us in all things except sin (Heb 4:15), we can only presume that he went through many of the goodbyes that other people his age experienced: growing pains of adolescence and self-identity, sorrowing over relatives who died, developing friendships and struggling with them, seeing his parents age, improving his work skills while sometimes failing at what he tried. Beyond these presumptions about his early years, we do know that leave-taking was a familiar part of the last three years of his life. It began with a goodbye to almost 30 years of security in his hometown, where a tug inside of him said, "It's time you moved on." It was time for him to walk away from everyone and everything that he had known—his home, his family, his friends, his work, his favorite places of recreation, relaxation and prayer, his at-homeness with the town and the surrounding area.

The walk away from his secure world took Jesus into a very significant rite of passage: his 40 days in the desert where he said a prayerful farewell to all those years of Nazareth and came to terms with the letting go that was being asked of him. He felt a power within himself that pulled him forth into a whole new world of ministry. Luke tells us that Jesus left the desert "with the power of the Spirit in him" (Lk 4:14). It was the power to say goodbye in order to say hello.

It was this power working in Jesus and the ever-deepening love of his Father that enabled Jesus to walk into the mobility and insecurity of his ministry. He who always had a place to lay his head for almost 30 years suddenly had no home, only a constant movement from one place to another (Lk 9:58). Life became one continual journey of deep investment and letting go, of rooting and uprooting, of settling down and of moving on. Even though Jesus was constantly on the go, however, he allowed himself to develop friendships, to love deeply, knowing it would mean the price of farewell. Some of the people with whom he invested his time and love were Mary, Martha and their brother Lazarus. They were good friends whose home in Bethany was a shelter and a comfort to him (Jn 11:1-2; 12:1-8; Lk 10:38-42). How renewed and rested he must have been after he had stopped there on his travels. Yet, Jesus knew he would have to get up and leave again after his visits. He could never just stay comfortable and secure in the place where he felt so at home, where he felt loved, respected, understood and accepted.

As Jesus got up and moved on, he met many who were experiencing loss in their lives: parents whose children had died, people who felt lost or rejected or were searching for truth, men and women who had known great emotional or physical pain, all kinds of people with all sorts of goodbyes wrapped around their hearts. Jesus showed compassion and he grieved with them. He often stopped along the way to comfort people in their hurts. He ached over their sufferings. "He took pity on them and healed their sick" (Mt 14:14). Jesus reached out and led them to hellos of good health, new vision of body or of spirit, to mental or emotional well-being, and to renewed inner life.

As he comforted others, Jesus continued to have his own farewells. His friend Mary tearfully told him of her brother's death, the brother whom Jesus greatly loved. The scriptures tell us that Jesus was so distressed that his sigh "came straight from the heart" and that he wept as he stood there before the tomb. So great was his sadness that those who stood nearby said, "See how much he loved him!" (Jn 11:36).

Jesus wept again in a very different situation. He was coming to Jerusalem, returning from a journey, possibly reflecting on his trip, on his hopes and longings for the people of his ministry. The yearning in his heart was so great that "as he drew near and came in sight of the city he shed tears over it and said, 'If you in your turn had only understood on this day the message of peace!' " (Lk 19:41-42). He lamented and was pained over all that he wanted for the people: "How often have I longed to gather your children, as a hen gathers her chicks under her wings, and you refused!" (Mt 23:37-38). It was a painful moment for Jesus as he dealt with yet another goodbye: He could not force the people to wake up to the truth of the kingdom. He had to let go of being able to do that. When I have heard parents weeping over children who have gone astray, when I have listened to the pain of church ministers who dreamed so much for a congregation that was immersed in its own selfish ambitions, when I have been with anyone who cried because the goodness they so intensely wanted to share had been rejected, I have thought of Jesus weeping over a people that refused to listen to his love and to change their ways.

Scripture does not tell us that Jesus wept over his cousin John's beheading, but it does imply that he needed time to grieve over the death of this good man for whom he had such high regard, the one of whom he said, "Of all the children born of women, a greater than John the Baptist has never been seen" (Mt 11:11). When Jesus received the news of John's death, "he withdrew by boat to a lonely place where they could be by themselves" (Mt 14:13). Tears of goodbye must have hung in the heart of Jesus as he grieved the going of his dear cousin.

There were all those other moments, too, when he had to let the grief stir inside, and just live with it and accept it. He said goodbye to respect by those in leadership and authority, to being understood by his disciples, and to being accepted by his own townspeople when he went home. It was these people of his own hometown who "sprang to their feet and hustled him out of town . . . intending to throw him down the cliff" (Lk 4:16-30). Yes, Jesus has been there before us in the hurt of rejection, non-acceptance and lack of understanding.

"The Emptied One"

All of these powerful events were part of the goodbye experience in the life of Jesus. Just as each of us has many daily losses throughout our life, so, too, with Jesus. And just as each of us has the large, significant, jolting, sometimes devastating goodbyes, so, too, with Jesus. It was the passion and death of Jesus which was the culmination and totality of his goodbyes, where his body and spirit were surrendered to the pain of leave-taking. He "emptied himself," letting go of all security and defenses, fully vulnerable to the pain of the human condition which was his (Phil 2:6-11).

As we reflect on this emptiness of Jesus, let us look at the Last Supper event. This scene is a goodbye holding many goodbyes. It was a farewell meal and speech to his friends; it was the terrible recognition that one of those dear to him was actually going to betray him, and that one of them would deny that he ever knew him. It was also the pain of coming nearer to his own death and it was a time when he could look back over his years of ministry, saying goodbye to all that he had not yet accomplished, remembering those he wept over as he approached Jerusalem.

All of these goodbyes were present but there was a unique and penetrating pain that took hold of Jesus that evening. It was an agonizing tension. On the one hand, he yearned to be with the "Abba" whose magnificent bonding claimed his heart, and on the other, he desired to be with those he loved so dearly through his life and ministry. Jesus knew the sadness and the ache in their hearts; he felt it keenly, and it only intensified his struggle with his own goodbyes. "One day when they were together in Galilee, Jesus said to them, 'The Son of Man is going to be handed over into the power of men; they will put him to death, and on the third day he will be raised to life again.' And a great sadness came over them" (Mt 17:22-23). The intense desire to be with his Father did not lessen the love which Jesus had for his friends. It only increased the ache within him as he felt the strain of departure coming upon him.

It was the powerful bond which Jesus had with his Abba that sustained him as he experienced the struggle of farewell. If Jesus had a one-liner that carried him through the emptiness of his goodbyes it had to be: *I am going to the Father* (Jn 14:12). Jesus' relationship with his father was one that grew and deepened and matured. He had come to know that he was truly the Beloved Son (Lk 3:22) and this vision centered in his heart, took a powerful hold on him, a truth that seared his depths with love. By the time that Jesus had reached that intense farewell of the last meal with his disciples, his yearning to be with his Father was a poignant, painful drawing in his heart. What tension was in him, wanting so much to complete that journey, yet struggling with paying the price of goodbye to get there.

Chapters 13 to 17 of John's gospel are filled with fragments of goodbye messages, beautiful speeches by Jesus where he attempts to have his disciples understand that he is leaving them, that the time has come for him to depart. They are the final goodbye messages of a dying one to the beloved. He expresses his love for them over and over again and tells them not to be afraid and troubled, but to be brave and to trust in the Father, to believe that they will one day be with him. Jesus calls them his dear friends and makes one final request that they carry on his work by loving one another. Time and again Jesus refers to the underlying strength in himself: "I am going to the Father" (Jn 14:28). "I am going to the one who sent me" (Jn 16:5). "As the Father has loved me . . ." (Jn 15:9). "The Father is with me" (Jn 16:32). Finally, he pours out his heart to his Father. Chapter 17 is a magnificent prayer of one who is coming to terms with having to pay the price of goodbye. He knows his hour has come as he reflects on his life. He stands before the Father, ready to give all, deeply desiring to go home:

> "I came from the Father and have come into the world
> and now I leave the world to go to the Father"
> (Jn 16:28).

> "Father, the hour has come . . .
> I am coming to you" (Jn 17:1, 11).

> "But now I am coming to you
> and while still in the world I say these things
> to share my joy with them to the full" (Jn 17:13).

Once Jesus had said his farewells and had braved the sadness of his last meal before his death, he went forth to walk the road of total abandonment. He knew he needed strength to endure the deep emptiness which awaited him. He needed time with his Father at one of his favorite prayer places. He asked his close friends to stand by him as he struggled with the pain. It was here in the olive garden that Jesus faced his fear of what lay ahead, begging the Father to spare him if he would, but always open to what would be. How much added intensity of pain it was for Jesus when his friends did not watch with him, did not stand by him as he agonized over the future. He loved them so totally and they would not be present to him when he most needed the comfort of a friend's just being there. Anytime we face our own agony of goodbyes and we have to go it alone without loved ones or friends to wait with us, we stand in the goodbye that Jesus stood in when he agonized before his death.

In the garden Jesus feared the inner void and pain that would be his. As he walked forth from there, he began to experience this. He received a shattering blow: the kiss of recognition from Judas (Lk 22:47-48). It is the goodbye kiss of anyone who has been betrayed by the one they deeply love. It is a sledgehammer affront to the ego and it rips apart the trust of one's heart. Jesus stood there and received the hello of Judas which was, in reality, filled with goodbye and death.

Long before Jesus reached the hill of Calvary he was bruised and torn by much psychic and physical pain. He had been betrayed by one friend and denied by another. He had been brutally beaten and treated as an inhuman object. He had seen the desolate compassion on his mother's face as he passed her by on the road and he had heard the jeers and taunts of those who despised him as he was lifted onto the cross.

As Jesus hung there dying, he was most surely like "the emptied one." Beneath him stood his beloved mother and a handful of friends with heartache and sorrow written on their faces. All the rest of his friends were "standing at a distance" (Lk 23:49). Inside of him the ache of goodbye went deeper and deeper as he thirsted and pained and cried out in agony to his Father. But even his Father seemed distant. Jesus, in his weak, broken, helpless condition, "cried out in a loud voice:

'My God, My God, why have you deserted me?' '' (Mt 27:46). This cry of the beloved Son is the cry of every person who has known a devastating goodbye in his or her life, when the overpowering feeling of aloneness, emptiness, desolation, abandonment, fills the human spirit. It is the inner cry: "Where are you, God, when I need you so much? Where are you? Why does this hurt so much? Why can't I feel your presence?" Jesus, the emptied one, bowed his head after a long, trailing lifetime of goodbyes and he surrendered to the deepest goodbye that anyone has ever known: "In a loud voice he said, 'Father, into your hands I commit my spirit.' With these words he breathed his last" (Lk 23:46).

Stand Strong in the Resurrection

If we were left with Jesus' emptiness and desolation, if we had only our kinship with him in his goodbyes, it would not be enough to sustain us in our own leave-taking. We would draw comfort, but we would not have the hope of a future hello. The beauty of the paschal mystery, the mystery of a passing over from death to life, of moving from goodbye to hello, is that it ends with hello. If Calvary is the deepest goodbye that anyone has ever known, then the resurrection is the greatest hello that anyone has ever proclaimed. The Father, the one whom Jesus treasured and with whom he yearned to be at home, surprised humanity and raised the Beloved from the dead.

Looking back on the resurrection experience, the disciples could say, "Now we understand . . . this is the green of the wheat seed that has fallen on the ground and died (Jn 12:24). This is the rejoicing that follows the mourning (Mt 5:5). This is the light after the dark-

ness (Jn 8:12). This is the blessing of taking up the cross
and following (Lk 9:18-27)." Their understanding of the
resurrection gave their world a different look. They could
hold bread and notice how it was broken before it was
shared; they could see the butterfly and remember the
truth of a torn and empty crysalis; they could awake in
the morning, feeling the sunlight warm upon their faces
and remember that dawn always follows the night. Jesus
was transformed. His risen presence with them transformed their world. They were never the same again. The
memory and reality of Jesus' death and resurrection had
put all of goodbye into perspective for them.

Jesus risen is a proclamation of "hello." He is a witness to us that when goodbyes do come that we can grow
through them. We can be changed, transformed. We can
be raised from our empty places of loss and can experience something new within us. Jesus risen proclaims:
"Stay close to the Father when you suffer from goodbyes.
Lean on this love and believe in his power to sustain you
and to raise you from your dark and lonely places."

We must take our suffering and always view it from
the perspective of the resurrection. We must look upon
our goodbyes from the direction of hello. We must stand
strong in the resurrection, believing that there is something beyond death, there is something beyond pain and
hurt and heartache. Here is where our strength and hope
lie. This is the power of the resurrection at work in us:

> *"Do not grieve like those who have no hope.*
> *We believe that Jesus died and rose again,*
> *and that it will be the same for those who*
> *have died in Jesus; God will bring them*
> *with him" (1 Thes 4:13-14).*

> *One black, rainy night as I lay awake*
> *in thunder's thud and lightning's splash,*

*I thought of the storms of life
that move through every human heart.*

*I pondered the mystery of suffering
while the dark night crashed and boomed,
and I thought about life's pain and grief
as my memory hung onto the resurrection.*

*The heavy rain found all the windows
and rinsed the house with its downpour,
and I remembered the flowers of the day
in the beauty of the fresh, green meadow.*

*How well the seasons speak to our hearts,
like a sacred gospel of the good earth,
telling us to believe in a hope-full God
who raised an entombed son from the dead.*

*In those moments when goodbyes cut deep
and old wounds rise up to hurt us,
when we get bent bearing others' burdens
or life seems destructive and unfair,
in these moments we need to look inward
to where the Easter vision warms us forever.*

*This is how we shall carry our sorrows,
this is how we shall bear our woundedness,
up against the great joy of the springtime
while standing strong in an empty tomb's truth.*

Creative Suffering

In Chapter 2 we reflected on "the value of suffering." Suffering in itself has no value. It is what we do with our suffering that makes the difference. The ministry of Jesus attests to this fact: He did all he could to alleviate the hurts of others. Yet, he also spoke of suffering as a source of growth, as a means of purification and inner conversion:

"I tell you most solemnly,
unless a wheat grain falls on the ground and dies,
it remains only a single grain;
but if it dies,
it yields a rich harvest" (Jn 12:24).

"Anyone who does not take up his cross and follow
in my footsteps is not worthy of me" (Mt 10:38).

"Happy those who mourn;
they shall be comforted.
Happy those who hunger and thirst for what is right;
they shall be satisfied. . . .
Happy those who are persecuted in the cause of right;
theirs is the kingdom of heaven" (Mt 5:5,6,10).

Suffering can be beneficial when it leads to some kind of "resurrection" in us, when a strength or a sleeping energy in us is aroused, when talents heretofore unknown are recognized, when a clarity about life's purpose and direction becomes keener for us, when a stronger sense of compassion for others deepens in us. There is so much within us that needs to come to life. Moments of suffering, times of goodbye, can cause us to peer inside our own tombs of unfinishedness or incompleteness and we can discover vast storehouses of resiliency, vitality, fidelity, love and endurance.

In Chapter 2 we also explored the false notion that God sends suffering to us in order to test us. God does not test us but the suffering that comes into our life because of our human condition can sear our spirit in such a way that we do become purer of heart, mellower, wiser, kinder, more understanding or devoted or compassionate. Suffering *can be* a refining or purifying element. Extreme suffering of body or spirit can send a person to deep inner recesses. It can be like the experience of a refinery where the heat of the furnace of life burns away the impurities. We can become like "gold tested in fire"—the best of who we are rises to the surface of our being. This aspect of suffering is noted in 1 Pt 1:6-7:

> You may for a short time have to bear being plagued by all sorts of trials; so that, when Jesus Christ is revealed, your faith will have been tested and proved like gold—only it is more precious than gold, which is corruptible even though it bears testing by fire.

The suffering of any goodbye, be it death or any other form of going away, can be a purification and a discipline in many ways. Things that we thought were important take on a totally different look: power or success or fame, to name a few. We learn the blessing of resiliency and the wonder of simple taken-for-granted things like getting out of bed without pain or going through a day without a tremendous deadness in our spirit.

When our suffering refines us in such a way that it leads to an inner change or transformation that positively affects our life or that of others, it becomes *creative suffering*. Jesus suffered creatively. His emptiness led to a radical transformation of new life. His risen presence lifted the hearts of those who met him and changed their lives.

When we suffer creatively, when a part of what was dead in us is raised to life, when something of us is refined and made purer, we go, like the risen Jesus, "to Galilee" (Mk 16:7). It is the Galilee of our own lives and we proclaim to others, mostly by our presence, that we have experienced hope and acceptance, that the emptiness and void within us have been filled with new life. We become enablers of life for ourselves and for others because there is something different about us and the way that we live. We have a changed perspective on life and we give others courage because we have been through a significant goodbye and have grown wiser and more tender.

Many times those who have suffered creatively become active sources of comfort and consolation for others. I have seen this often in those I have met. I saw creative suffering clearly evident in a woman I know, a mother of eight children. She had severe back problems and wore a body cast for a year. She was almost completely helpless, with intense pain constantly. When I met her she was struggling with depression and self-pity. She felt that she needed to "go deeper," to learn to pray with the scriptures so that she could draw strength from an interior source. She felt so little physical or spiritual strength at that time. She also wanted to learn how to keep a prayer journal. During those years I watched her grow deeper and more valiant. Even when she finally threw away her body cast, there was still never a day that passed without pain in her back. This woman became a different person in many ways. People were drawn to her because they sensed a powerful courage in her and they knew that she could help them in their distress just by listening to them. She who had not known how to look up a scripture passage a few years before began to help others to pray in this way. She who had never written in a journal was encouraging others to try this helpful approach in their lives. She had experienced a difficult goodbye, but she was raised to life. She continues this day to be a blessing of hope to others who are going through their own suffering.

On a journey to St. Louis I met a blind man. I shall never forget him. He, too, greatly influenced my understanding of what it means to suffer creatively. He was a young, handsome man, wounded in Vietnam. He had spent his days since then helping blind college students cope with life, encouraging them to appreciate all the opportunities that were theirs and showing them how to live as an unsighted person. His enthusiasm about life was contagious. As he spoke, I felt I was in the presence of someone who had come through the fire and was pure gold. His appreciation of people and life was wonderful. As I walked off the plane in St. Louis I knew that another seed of hope had been deeply planted in my heart by this messenger of God.

There are so many people like these two who have suffered creatively. They are the ones who walk in the footsteps of the risen Jesus. They carry the truth of resurrection in hearts which have been emptied and refilled. They know that farewells and goodbyes are not forever when one lives with faith in the eternal hello. People who have suffered creatively, who have taken their pain of body or spirit and are united with the emptied one who was raised from the dead, know that when a child grows up, when a friend moves away, when a loved one dies, it does not have to be the end. They believe that there will be growth, change, newness. They are grateful and rejoice in the love-bond that unites them with that child-now-grown, that friend moving on, that dying one coming into fullness of life. Their faith and their lives profess this belief: "I think that what we suffer in this life (the goodbyes) can never be compared to the glory (the hello) as yet unrevealed which is waiting for us" (Rom 8:18).

Thus it is that whenever it is time for goodbyes, for leaving behind and for moving on, I think of Jesus. I think of how many goodbyes he said, how many farewell tears he wiped away, how many hellos he walked into, how many risks of moving on he accepted. I think of Jesus, always traveling on in his years of ministry, stopping to catch his breath and his heart in mountain moments with the Father whose love was drawing him home. I think of Jesus, letting go, with a faithful belief in the pattern of hello-goodbye-hello. I think of Jesus, the emptied one, brought into fullness of life by a loving God. I think of Jesus, purely pilgrim "with nowhere to lay his head," and I think of us, taking up and following.

Questions for Reflection, Integration, Discussion:

1. What do you consider to be the most difficult part of Jesus' journey of life?

2. When you reflect upon the life and message of Jesus, what is the most helpful aspect for you in facing your own farewells?

3. Where do you find hope in your goodbye times?

4. Have you known people who have suffered creatively? If yes, who are they and what are some of the characteristics of their growth in suffering?

5. Read/pray Chapters 14-17 of John's gospel. Circle words in these chapters which seem to relate particularly to your own losses. What ideas, feelings, came to you as you read and prayed these chapters?

CHAPTER FOUR

❖

Like a Flock of Homesick Cranes

> Like a flock of homesick cranes
> flying night and day back to
> their mountain nests, let all my
> life take its voyage to its eternal
> home in one salutation to thee.
>
> —Rabindranath Tagore

What do homesick cranes have to do with goodbyes and with the broken places of our lives? They are a symbol of our inside, the place that I call the pilgrim heart. It is a part of us that is never home, that is always stretching and yearning to be home but knows that we have not yet arrived. It is the yearning that was in Jesus, the broken one, as he was drawn home to be with his Father. Jesus was one of the homesick cranes and his winging homeward is a process that each one of us experiences. It is the journey of our spirit and the road markers along the way keep saying: HELLO this way, GOODBYE that way. When we recognize this faith dimension of our lives, it can make the necessity of goodbyes a little easier to understand and can help us to live through the pain of our heartaches with more hope. We can see our life experiences from the perspective of going home, and we can know that the groaning and yearning of our spirits is natural because we are in the homeward process.

Because we are pilgrims whose homeland is not here, we journey, search, travel, discover, live with mystery, doubt and wonder. We see dreams come true; we see hopes alive. We see dreams dashed; we see hopes die. We start over again—with people, work, prayer, our whole life, all the days of our life. It is the way of the human spirit. Journey has become a very common word in the vocabulary of many people. It implies that we are going somewhere, that we are on the road traveling to a particular destination. In our mobile society, we take many journeys in our lifetime. Sometimes the destination is as close as a neighbor's doorstep or the local grocery store. At other times, it is as far away as another continent where there is little that is familiar to us. Journey is also used in reference to the traveling that we do on the inside of ourselves, where there is a greater vastness and unfamiliarity than the physical continent far away from us.

The journey inside always has the aura of mystery and challenge because when we travel inward we can see only with the eyes of faith. We must believe in the value of that inner road and trust that it will lead us to places in the heart that are waiting to bless us with their truth and beauty. It is much like exploring a mountain trail that one has never been on before. We walk along (sometimes huffing and puffing) and many times we pause and take another path or turn around and go back, thinking that the trail is either too ordinary or too hard or too long for us to continue. If we had just gone around the next bend and up the hill, we might have come to a magnificent vista of beauty. It is in this journey of the spirit that we enter into a pattern that is often repeated: We let go of the way we have known, we lose the way, we search for the way, and we find the way. We continually seek meaning in life and ponder the course of our inner direction. We keep coming upon facets of self-truth in us that we never knew existed.

Our goodbyes can compel us to enter this pattern. They can lead us into deeper, newer territory if only we will continue, even when the going gets rough or the path seems unsure and we want to give up.

If we do choose to continue the journey inward, we can never settle down in a newly found place for very long. These places are only temporary dwellings. They are havens of comfort, however, and they remind us that at the core of our being there is an eternal dwelling place of peace. But we must always move on because we are never finished, not as long as we are on this side of life. We are always in the process of getting there, of going home. If we are open and reflective as we continue the path inward, we keep discovering more and more inner vistas and places that we never knew existed. These are the markers toward peace. Sometimes when we discover them we say ''Ah!'' for the beauty we have found; sometimes we exclaim ''Ouch!'' in our pain of the truth; and sometimes we give a recognizing ''Oh!'' for the depths to which we have come. These discoveries are sign-posts to continue on and we do so because we know that we are nomads who keep journeying, making our way through the hellos and the goodbyes of our travels. As we go along our way, we have tastes of our eternal home of everlasting peace, but these are brief, only appetizers. Sometimes we think that we are there, we feel so secure and so confident and so loving, but then life breaks all this loose and we find ourselves again searching for the meaning in life and yearning for peace. We realize once more that we are still far from home, that place of forever hello.

And where is the place of forever hello? It is the place of our own wholeness of self, that inner core of peace. It is also the place of being in the heart of God. The paradox is that when we enter the home of our God, we also enter the home of our true self. There is no more false self in us. We come home to ourselves in our wholeness, our goodness, our fullness of beauty. We know clearly and completely, for the first time, that we are truly made in the image and likeness of God.[1] The radiance of divine goodness blends and joins our own inner light and tranquility and we know, in truth, that we are one. This homecoming is always in process. It is fulfilled in that meeting on the other side of life— eternity. But the deeper we go on our inward journey in this present life, the more we enter into the truth of this oneness. The greater our love of this God whose home is our own, the greater will be the yearning and longing in our hearts to be with God. We, too, will be the homesick cranes who are winging our way to the home-land. The goal will burn so brightly and deeply in the core of our beings that we will fly night and day back to our mountain nests, making our voyage with great expectation and longing.

Whether we recognize it or not, there is a homesick crane in each of us. Some of us are flying at great speed and intensity and some of us are still sitting in the marshland trying to find the courage to take off. The homesick crane in us knows that life is a journey, that we can never completely settle down and settle in, be-cause "home is the place we are always going to but never arrive."[2] The homesick crane in us is the pilgrim who never arrives, who is always going home, some-times not having any idea of which way to turn but knowing deep within that there is a goal awaiting and

1. Thomas Merton, *New Seeds of Contemplation* (N.Y.: New Di-rections, 1972), pp. 29–36.
2. Alla Bozarth-Campbell, Ph.D., *Life Is Goodbye, Life Is Hello:* Grieving Well Through All Kinds of Loss (Minneapolis, MN: CompCare, 1982), p. 89.

that it is well worth the journey with all its ups and downs, with all its hellos and goodbyes.

The tension that comes from being a homesick crane is that while we know that we are always going home, we must also be deeply rooted and involved in our present condition. We, like Jesus, must invest ourselves as totally as possible in loving others and in being loved by them. We must give ourselves to the human journey and not try to by-pass it because it is in and through our humanness that we discover the beauty of the inner terrain. It is through this that we are transformed into who we are meant to be. It is through this that we unite with the heart of God.

In *The Problem of Pain*, C. S. Lewis stresses the longing for home in his chapter on heaven:

> There have been times when I think we do not desire heaven but more often I find myself wondering whether, in our heart of hearts, we have ever desired anything else.[3]

The early Christians had a strong sense of this heaven within them. The author of the letter to the Hebrews fills chapter 11 with models of faith, people whose pilgrim-heart attitudes carried them through the difficult times of their lives. The fact that they believed their home was not here is made very clear:

> All these died in faith, before receiving any of the things that had been promised, but they saw them in the far distance and welcomed them, recognizing that they were only strangers and nomads on earth. People who use such terms about themselves make it quite plain they are in search of their real homeland.

3. C. S. Lewis, *The Problem of Pain* (N.Y.: Macmillan, 1944), p. 133.

They can hardly have meant the country they came
from, since they had the opportunity to go back to
it, but in fact they were longing for a better homeland, their heavenly homeland (Heb 11:13-16).

The Groaning Within Us

As we long for our heavenly homeland, as we yearn
for a deep center of peace in which to settle, we can
feel within our spirits a groaning and an ache much like
that of giving birth. For, as our pilgrim spirits mature,
as they gestate and come into wholeness, they are filled
with birth pangs, with the labor of letting go, with the
struggle of new life which has been forming in us. The
groaning within is especially intense when we experience certain forms of loss and brokenness. Adult transitions, confusion about who we are (particularly at
mid-life), loss of deep relationships, desert prayer and
darkness, harsh encounters with our false self or sinfulness, the pain of giftedness or creativity, all of these
changes and challenges create a deep groaning in the
human spirit, a crying out of the souls as one goes
deeper.

This going deeper always involves a leaving behind.
We cannot go deeper unless we let go of the place we
have known. To descend into the depths of ourselves
we must be willing to risk losing the security and the
safety of that to which we have become so accustomed.
It may mean leaving behind a certain self-image or some
deeply rooted concepts, such as our understanding of
what it means to be church or to be masculine or feminine, of what it means to be family or friend, of what
it means to be successful or whole.

When we are experiencing the groaning within us—
those webs of confusion or disorientation or loss—when
our life appears to be filled with failure and ungained
dreams, when darkness looms up large against the tiny
light of our hope, when our inner poverty gasps for a
touch of fullness, when our brokenness cries out to be
mended, it is then that our groaning is met with the
Spirit of God who groans within us (Rom 8:18-23; 2
Cor 5:1-5). It is this God of life who blesses our inner
birthing, standing by us, urging us to stay in the process, filling us with energy by the intimate touch of an
eternal love shared with us.

All Is on Loan

What gives us the courage to stay with the groaning
of our spirit? What keeps us winging our way homeward? How do we not clutch and cling to our securities
and to all that we have come to know and to cherish?
There is an ancient Aztec Indian prayer that reflects on
the preciousness of life and the fleetingness of it. As
the Aztecs thank the Creator for their life and breath,
they acknowledge that they are only on loan to each
other for a short while, and just like the drawings that
they have made in crystalline obsidian fade, so, too,
will their life quickly be gone.

> *Oh,* only for so short a while you
> have loaned us to each other,
> *because we take form in your act*
> *of drawing us,*
> *And we take life in your painting us,*
> *and we breathe in your singing us.*

But only for so short a while
have you loaned us to each other.[4]

This "on loan" philosophy is the first and most important attitude of a pilgrim heart. It can give us the courage to stay with the groaning of our spirit. It can carry us through many a hard time and can help us to hold our treasures in open hands when we want so much to resist the letting go of them. When we look upon all of life as being on loan to us, we look at it differently. We look at this loan for what it is—purely gift, given to us out of love. We reverence all that we have and take great joy in it, but we do not grasp, cling to, or hoard our treasures.

There is always a deep gratitude in those who look upon all of life as gift. As Isaiah 55 describes it, we do not earn what is given; it is simply there for us to receive and we do so in thanksgiving and in awe.

Oh, come to the water all you who are thirsty;
though you have no money, come!
Buy corn without money, and eat,
and, at no cost, wine and milk. . . .
Listen. Listen to me . . . and your soul will live
(Is 55:1-3).

Thus, we look at our world and its people through the eyes of a child caught up in wonder and we approach it and care for it with all the commitment and tenderness of a responsible adult, knowing that it is only given to us for a time.

Deep down we know that all is on loan to us. Life does change and sometimes so quickly. Accidents happen, disease spreads, storms come, aging continues, jobs terminate, mistakes occur. We go to bed one eve-

4. Ancient Aztec Indian Prayer, Source unknown.

ning feeling good about life and ourselves. We awake in the morning and during the course of that day our world can be turned upside down by news of the death of a loved one, or an unexpected rift in a friendship, or the loss of a priceless possession, or a doctor's prognosis, or an unexpected financial decision. All of life is filled with loss and with letting go. For the one who believes that all is on loan, this is to be expected. Not that this expectation cripples the spirit of joy. Just the opposite is true; the present moment is treasured and enjoyed all the more because it is so precious and so fleeting. Those whose days have been numbered by an incurable illness will attest to this fact; suddenly the truth of life being on loan becomes a piercing reality and they are intensely aware of how fragile and beautiful it is.

Love will go with us on our journey home. Knowing that all is on loan enables us not to fight so much when we are asked to let go, because we realize that those we cherish, while a wonderful blessing to us, cannot be kept from going home. The focus is on life and love, not on death and disaster, because the Christian pilgrim knows that the one thing that does last forever is love. This love is on permanent loan to us because the Abba, whose beckoning catches our homesick hearts, is love. Our faith assures us that all those we hold dearly in our hearts will meet us on the other side and together we will celebrate the wonder of this treasure. It is joy, not sorrow, that Christian pilgrims carry in their hearts, because they know that they are on their way to their home in this God who is love.

The on loan attitude pervades other aspects of being a pilgrim. One of these is realizing that we can never return to a place and expect to find it the same. When we do go back, we are changed from the time we were first there and many times the place we return to is also different. I remember one time on retreat having a very sacred place of prayer on a sandbar in the Platte River. It was a wonderful spot of beauty and inspiration. A year later I went back to celebrate the wonders of my retreat days, expecting to find the sandbar and to relive the feelings of my retreat days. Neither occurred. The sandbar was gone and I did not feel the special bondedness of the year before. We can celebrate the past but we cannot hang on to it and expect it to remain just as it was for us. When we keep going back to our past, either in memory or in reality, and always wishing life could be "the way it was then," we are clinging too tightly. Sometimes we need to stay in the past for a while until we are healed of some of the hurt of letting go, but eventually it is time to move on. Pilgrim hearts must invest in the present and look down the road with the strength of good memories pressing them forward.

Many times I have asked people in my classes to think about what they would pack in their "suitcase of life"—what the essentials were for them as they pilgrimaged through life. Doing this tells a lot about who and what one values in life. One of the most needed items that ought to be in our suitcase of life is courage. Pilgrims simply must take risks. They do not always know where they are going. Not to take risks keeps us from many experiences that lead to growth. Fear can keep us from going up that high hill to a vista of beauty and a whole new approach to existence. It can keep the birthing from happening in us. It can keep the emptiness from being filled.

Finally, the pilgrim heart learns to recognize and to cope with the demons along the way, those elements of life that pull us into darkness, discouragement and self-pity. They can become so strong that we fall by the roadside and feel that we can never rise again. The demons which we encounter can eat away at our self-esteem, cause us to question our own goodness or the goodness of life, and create a great anxiety about the future. We lose hope of recovery, of moving on, and we think that we simply cannot do what is asked of us in our moment of goodbye. The journey just seems too much for us.

The Exodus in Us

When pilgrim hearts are anxious and hurting from their journey and its struggles, it is sometimes difficult to name and to fight the demons along the way. I have often encouraged pilgrim hearts who were facing long stretches of inner wilderness filled with discouragement and doubt to read and to pray the book of Exodus. Many can identify with the journey of the Israelites as they moved out of their land of slavery, across the fearsome and harsh terrain of the desert, to the Promised Land. The Exodus is the story of every pilgrim heart because there is always the movement from a place of non-freedom to a place of true freedom.

The pilgrim heart stands in a position similar to the Exodus travelers and knows that there will always be an Egypt that needs a goodbye. All these goodbyes call to us to not be held captive. The people of the Exodus were as human and as vulnerable as we are today. They did not like uprooting any more than we do. Even though their life in Egypt was filled with brokenness, in many ways it was hard for the Israelites to accept the conditions for moving on. It meant leaving behind all that they had ever known and most of their possessions to face an unknown and uncertain passage which

Deuteronomy calls "the vast and terrible wilderness" (Dt 1:19). They left so quickly that they "carried off their dough, still unleavened, on their shoulders, their kneading bowls wrapped in their cloaks" (Ex 12:34). So distraught and uprooted were they that later, when Moses shared God's promises of future freedom with them, they would not listen to him. It is difficult for anyone going through brokenness to feel and to believe that down the road all will be well, that God will provide. And because the feelings are not there, they often begin to lash out at life or to give up, as the Israelites did.

Secondly, it is easy to give in to grumbling on the journey. Over and over the people of Israel brought their complaints to Moses: "You have brought us to this wilderness to starve this whole company to death. . . . Why did you bring us out of Egypt? . . . Was it so that we should die of thirst?" And they "put Yahweh to the test by saying: 'Is Yahweh with us or not?' " (Ex 16:2-3; 17:3,7). We often do the same when we go through our own wilderness. We won't let go of what we have known, what we are used to, so we miss the manna, the nourishment offered to us in our present condition. We ignore the treasure of friends, the power of prayer, the beauty of our own goodness, the hope of new life offered to us, or the truth that will set us free.

Yet another similarity in the Israelite's journey is that they had to take the roundabout way instead of the road that was nearest and most direct for them:

> When Pharaoh had let the people go, God did not let them take the road to the land of the Philistines, although that was the nearest way. God thought that the prospect of fighting would make the people lose heart and turn back to Egypt. Instead, God led the

people by the roundabout way of the wilderness . . .
(Ex 13:17).

As we journey along, we sometimes find that we are
caught in detours or sideroads of life that seem useless
or futile. But when we look back we see that the roundabout way was a valuable one. Although we never would
have chosen it, we have discovered deeper wisdom because of this side step on our journey.

Just as pilgrim hearts cannot settle down forever, neither could the Israelites. They had camped at the Sea
of Reeds and found that it was a good, comfortable
place. Exodus 15:22 states that they wanted to stay there
but Moses pressed them to move on. This action is re-
affirmed in Deuteronomy: "You have stayed long
enough at this mountain: move on from here. Continue
your journey" (Dt 1:6). All of us have a basic need for
security but if we are on our way home then we, too,
can never stay at our cozy place when we are challenged
by life to go forward on the inner journey.

In noting the similarities of the Israelites' journey
with that of the pilgrim heart, the most strengthening
and hopeful aspect of the book of Exodus is the faithful,
caring presence of God with those who journeyed
through the wilderness. This truth is evident from the
very first: "God heard their groaning. . . . I am well
aware of their sufferings" (Ex 2:23; 3:7). It is a truth
that is repeated throughout the long journey. God constantly reassures them of his strengthening and protec-
tive presence:

> *"I shall be with you. . . . I have visited you. . . .*
> *I will free you of the burdens. . . .*
> *I will release you from slavery. . . .*
> *I will adopt you as my own people,*
> *and I will be your God"* (Ex 3:12, 16; 6:6-7).

Finally, just as the pilgrims must recognize the demons along the way, so too must great attention be given to the messengers from God who encourage us and guide us. The scriptures are filled with stories of magnificent carriers of God's word. In our day they are still strongly present among us. These messengers come most often in human form: They could be a best friend or a stranger on the street. They could be the voice of a child or the words penned in a letter by one who cares. These messengers may not know that they are carrying the word of God to us but they are. For God, in a great desire to comfort us, has moved within their beings and brought them to us in our wilderness of grief.

The attitude of a pilgrim heart will change the way we live through our times of Exodus and will help us to walk into the goodbyes that await us. We may still hurt deeply because, as Christian pilgrims, we give our hearts in love and choose to invest ourselves in life just as Jesus did; but we will approach the hurt in a different way. We will have hope that "what we suffer in this life can never be compared to the glory, as yet unrevealed, which is waiting for us" (Rom 8:18). We will have courage to go on because we know that there is more to life than just what we have experienced here on earth. We will not be grasping for or clinging to people or things; there will be a deeper appreciation of them because we know that we do not own them but only have them for a time.

Whatever our present situation in life, we are Exodus people. Whether we are in Egypt, in the middle of the wilderness, or close to the Promised Land, whether we are engulfed in the grief process or are overjoyed with new life, whether we are in a painful or exciting process of self-discovery, whether we are coping with severe loss or are at a cozy place, we carry pilgrim hearts within us. This truth marks our lives with hello and goodbye.

Inwardly, life's events will constantly ask of us the question, "Where have you come from and where are you going?" (Gn 16:8). As Christian pilgrims we can respond, "We are on our way home. We have come from journeys filled with hello and goodbye. In the midst of our joys and sorrows, we know that all is gift and that we have a God whose faithful presence radiates love and hope to us."

The more we set our hearts on this God, the more our hearts will yearn and long for a place with God. The homesick crane in us will deepen in intensity and clarity and will give the determination and the freedom we need to keep winging our way homeward. And so we can say to each one we meet along the way, "Walk with us, we need your courage. Stand by us, we need strength. Smile upon us often, we need love. For it is never easy, this wilderness journey of groaning, and we often grow weary with the winging."

Questions for Reflection, Integration, Discussion

1. When have you most felt like "a homesick crane"?

2. Are there any characteristics of a pilgrim heart that give you hope and encouragement? If yes, which ones?

3. What would you pack in your suitcase of life?

4. What does the attitude of "all is on loan" say to you about your present situation in life?

5. Which of the aspects of the Exodus most speaks of your own pilgrim journey? (You may wish to read the book of Exodus with these aspects in mind.)

CHAPTER FIVE

✦

Praying Our Goodbyes

> At every turn in the road a new illumining is
> needed to find the way and a new kindling is
> needed to follow the way.
>
> —John S. Dunne

I remember so well the day I went to the home of a
family whose teenage daughter had been killed in a car
accident. It was a moment full of deep sorrow and I
knew that it would be no easy visit. Helen took me to
her daughter's bedroom. There, on the bed, she had
placed all of the major mementos of her daughter's few
and swift school years. I remember especially the school
jacket with a bright, shiny medal she had won the day
before she died. Helen pointed out the mementos and
spoke both proudly and poignantly of her daughter's
short but full life. We stood there bonded in silent sadness, tears in our eyes and hearts. Then we joined the
other members of the family and friends who had gathered. Each one who entered the home was greeted in
this same manner.

Now, many years later, as I reflect on that visit, I
realize what a beneficial ritual that was. It never occurred to me at the time that Helen was praying a goodbye; but looking back on it, I see how she was doing
exactly that. Each time she escorted another visitor to
the room and stopped to ponder, she was living out the
pain of her daughter's death. The mementos of her

daughter were the images that Helen needed to link her with the child she had birthed, nurtured and deeply loved, the child she had swiftly lost in a blur of tragic time.

When we pray a goodbye our focus is on hurt and healing. Many times it is just a first step, or a beginning of the process of being healed. At other times it can be a very profound movement of healing in the heart of the one who grieves. It may feel like opening a window and airing a stuffy room, or like finding the key to a door that has long been closed. It may seem like finally discovering the right medication for a lengthy ailment.

There are four aspects of praying a goodbye: recognition, reflection, ritualization and reorientation. When we actually pray a goodbye the elements merge into one another and are not so easily separated as they are described later in this chapter. There may also be times when all four aspects are not present, but usually when we pause to bring our pain to prayer we can find them.

The four elements can be found in Helen's farewell to her daughter. Helen certainly *recognized* or named the deep pain of loss which came with her daughter's death. She used the mementos and the walk to the bedroom to *ritualize* that deep hurt. As she and her guests paused by the bed to *reflect* in silence, they began connecting the loss within them to the mystery of God and the human condition. The process of healing or *reorientation* was nurtured at that time. Helen was indeed praying her goodbye.

Prayer and the Experience of Goodbye

Since this experience of many years ago, I have grown in my perception of what prayer is and in my understanding of the grieving process. This has greatly influenced my approach. I now realize that prayer is so much more than "talking to God" or reciting formal prayers or having good feelings about God. I have learned, too, that our prayer takes on a whole different look when we are experiencing the loss of someone or something highly significant in our lives. Grief has a way of plundering our prayer life, leaving us feeling immobile and empty. The experience of deep loss is that inner turn on the road of life of which John Dunne speaks. It is a time when we search for a light to find our way. We cry out for a "new kindling" to burn within us so that we will have a desire and a reason to continue forward on the road of life.

All of us have those turns in the road. It is what we do or do not do with them that makes the difference. All too often we can let a life transition sit in our soul, discomfort us, empty us, discourage us and sometimes strangle us with its strong, clenching hold. Too often we can ignore a goodbye or fight it or push it away, but we do not get rid of the ache in this way. It keeps raising its voice inside us, at times when we least expect. It drowns out the voice of joy in our life, bleeds our spirit of energy and enthusiasm; it destroys belief in our ability to rise from the ashes of our pain.

We need to acknowledge the ache of our goodbyes and to approach them in a way that leads to personal growth. When we pray a goodbye we do more than just pray *about* loss. Praying about it is to keep it out there, apart from us in some sense. When we truly pray a goodbye we enter into the whole matter; we live it. We connect our life with God and bring our pain into that intimate relationship, and know that the touch of God is the touch of healing (''Power came out of him that cured them all'' Lk 6:19).

When we pray, we enter into a process of communicating with God, believing in our deepest being that this communication makes a difference in our lives. Good communication between persons always goes both ways—each listens and each responds. So, too, with God and us. Sometimes we speak and sometimes we listen and sometimes there is a lot said without any words coming between the two of us. The wonder of our communion with God is that it can happen anywhere and anytime. Sometimes this event is as simple as seeing the morning star shine upon us and sensing a deep bonding with the magnificent Creator. Other times it is as deliberate as a structured meditation time, or as deep as a moment of intense, intimate silence. And sometimes it is as penetrating as the cry of agony which dwells in a heart full of pain. However it is that we communicate with God, and God with us, the truth is that God is deeply involved in our lives, touching us with love. This touch of God is the touch of transformation. We can never walk closely with God for very long and not have this presence make a difference in our lives, although we may not feel or see that difference for a long time.

It is one of the great ironies of our human condition that at the time when we most need to experience the tender compassion and strengthening comfort of our God, we very often feel a great distance in this relationship. The closeness or the sense of presence may not be felt. The desire and the energy to pray are gone. It is as though the human spirit has shriveled up, gone dry and been swallowed in the darkness of heartache and the sawdust of sorrow. A tiny, weak voice in us calls us to pray but our tired, empty minds and hearts have no desire to respond. It takes us time to readjust to loss and change. It is much like plants that are moved from one environment to another; they are stunned for weeks, even months, before they respond to their new surroundings and begin to grow and bloom again. It may take the one in grief a long time before she or he feels like praying.

The psalmist echoed the emptiness of the people in exile with this lament: "How could we sing a song to the Lord in a foreign land?" (Ps 137:4, NAB). Indeed, it is difficult for anyone who feels alien from self, life, others, or God to sing a song to the Lord. Our prayer is greatly influenced by what our bodies and our spirits are experiencing. When we do not have a desire to pray, it does not mean that we have lost our faith or that we are being unfaithful to God or that God has forsaken us. Rather, it means that we are experiencing loss, and are at the bend in the road, feeling drained, hollow, empty, spent.

That is why our faith and prayer every single day is so important. It enables us to develop a strong union with God. We deepen our roots of love as we seek an ever more enduring communion in daily prayer. Then, when times of loss are weighing heavily on our hearts and we do not have a felt sense of God's presence, we can fall back on the steadfast belief that God always keeps vigil over us. ("Yahweh kept vigil to bring them out of the land of Egypt. . . ." Ex 12:42).

It is also very helpful during times of darkness and emptiness to have scripture verses that are comforting and soothing to our aching spirit. We need to have our spiritual one-liners (cf. Chapter 2) that we can rely on to get us through the tough times. Some scriptural one-liners that are often balm to my woundedness are:

I know the plans I have in mind for you . . . plans
for peace, not disaster, reserving a future full of hope
for you (Jer 29:11).

I have loved you with an everlasting love (Jer 31:3).

Only goodness and kindness shall follow me, all the
days of my life (Ps 23:6, NAB).

There is nothing I cannot master with the help of
the One who gives me strength (Phil 4:13).

I shall look for the lost one, bring back the stray,
bandage the wounded and make the weak strong
(Ez 34:16).

Do not let your hearts be troubled (Jn 14:1).

It is especially difficult to pray when a person is very
ill, particularly if one has been receiving medication
for pain. Remembered one-liners can be a comfort in
great pain, but sometimes even this is not possible. A
woman who had an extensive hospital stay due to cancer
surgery told me how she just could not pray during
those intense days. But she took great solace in the fact
that her community of friends and family were praying,
not just praying *for* her, but praying in her place. "How
comforting," she said to me, "to know that the community is at prayer even though I cannot pray." She
surrendered in peace to this fact and let go of her guilt
and frustration in being unable to turn her mind and
heart to things of God. (Surely her will to pray and her
acceptance and joy of the community at prayer were in
themselves wonderful prayers of faith and love.)

No matter how strong our faith, though, and no matter how deep our love of God and others, there may be
moments (maybe days, months) in our grieving when it

feels like we just "go through the motions" of prayer and that all is aimless and worthless. But this is a very necessary part of our spiritual growth. It is the fallow time, the winter time, the barren time. It is the seedtime for us, the dark of the earth before the greening, and we must continue to throw our empty selves into God's arms, leaning on this stronghold, and trusting that the power of healing is going on in us because this is the only way to springtime. It is true of the earth and it is true of us. God never leaves us during our winters of the heart.

When we want to give up on God because we have lost our desire to pray and do not have a feeling of God's nearness, we need to remember that God understands us and accepts us in our sadness which is part of the human condition. At these times God says to us: "Keep believing in the greening, in the springtime of your heart. I know that it feels as though I am far away from you but I am closer to you than your next breath. On your weary days, just come and sit by the well of life with me. I will stay with you. On your discouraged days, remember that I yearn to fill your life with joy. It will return to you in time. On your days when you feel the ache will never go away, press your pain against me and know that I surround you with an everlasting love. Draw your strength and energy from me. I will sustain you in this wintry, dark time."

How Do We Pray a Goodbye?

One way we pray a goodbye is through the funeral or memorial service which the church wisely provides for those who grieve the death of a loved one. But funerals and memorial services are not enough. First, they do not provide for grieving the many other kinds of loss in our lives such as divorce or adult transition. Secondly, we need more than a one-time prayer to be healed of our loss. Grieving goes on long after the funeral is over. We need ongoing prayer to sustain us and heal us day by day.

The approach I have developed for praying our goodbyes is to use the four aspects mentioned above: recognition, reflection, ritualization and reorientation. The four parts of the process are developed in the following portions of this chapter and are used in the prayers of the final section of the book.

1. *Recognition*

We begin by identifying or naming the loss that we have experienced. We also name the hurt or pain that has been ours because of this experience. This is a moment of honesty for ourselves as we enter into the prayer process. It sounds simple enough to do, but some people walk around hurting for a long time before they identify their inner woundedness. Recently a woman in her 50s was feeling a great restlessness and a deep anxiety about life. She eventually was able to name the loss that was hers due to early retirement and expressed a feeling of freedom and peace in knowing that this was a very natural response for her to have. Another woman shared with me her discovery of how stoical she had been about her father's death. She was the youngest in her family and had a close relationship with him. She had not realized how deeply she had buried her sadness because everyone else in her family appeared to be so strong in accepting the death. Once she acknowledged her gulf of grief she, too, knew she was free to take the next step in being healed of the hurt.

Naming the goodbye and the hurt may add to our pain

initially because we see how real it is, but it is a necessary first step. Some helps for identifying our goodbyes and the hurts of our grieving have been given in Chapter 1. These questions would be a good place to begin as one is recognizing or naming the pain of loss.

2. *Reflection*

The second step in praying a goodbye is one that our Western culture does not encourage and one which many adults need to develop on all levels of life: taking time to reflect. To give ourselves to reflection is to become comfortable with slowing down, with stillness, with solitude and aloneness, with not being afraid to look inward or to go deeper. In many ways our Western world says: "Use all the time you have to keep busy, be successful and make money; do as much as you can as fast as you can; ignore the simple beauties in life and grab onto complexity; live for yourself and by all means, do everything you can to run away from and to avoid hurt of any kind. If you have to grieve, do it in a hurry and then get on with life." Ours is a culture where life is lived on the surface, a life lived on the run with many fast food places to complement it. The inner world, the place of depth and meaning, the core of our being where God dwells, is all too easily missed or ignored. Because of this, many people have not disciplined their lives to include spaces of time where they do nothing except ponder, wonder, listen and be still.

This part of praying a goodbye can, then, be very difficult for those who are unaccustomed to taking time for reflection. They may be very uncomfortable with the quiet that it requires. Once they place themselves in this part of the process, however, it can be tremendously fruitful for them. In this second step, we take the hurt of the loss which we have identified, and we give it our full attention. We sit with it, look at it, face it, even though it grieves us to do so. One of the values of this prayerful reflection is that it enables us to discover our deeper feelings and to reconnect our lives with God. Sometimes we may be "too nice" with God. We can hide our true feelings because we do not want to shock or offend God or have God think ill of us. We do not want to admit that we are capable of such feelings. We need to let God hear our cry and our distress. God knows it anyhow! Let God hear our anger and our confusions, our frustrations and our disorientation. Let God know that we wish things would change for us or that things were different. The people of scripture have much to tell us about getting feelings out in the open with God. The author of *Lamentations* encourages:

> *Up, cry out in the night-time,*
> *in the early hours of darkness;*
> *pour your heart out like water*
> *before Yahweh (Lam 2:19).*

The psalms are filled with honest cries of grief and anguish:

> *How much longer must I endure grief*
> *in my soul,*
> *and sorrow in my heart by day and by*
> *night? (Ps 13:2)*

> *Take pity on me, Yahweh,*
> *I am in trouble now.*
> *Grief wastes away my eye,*
> *my throat, my inmost parts.*
> *For my life is worn out with sorrow,*
> *my years with sighs (Ps 31:9-10).*

I am like water draining away,
  my bones are all disjointed,
my heart is like wax,
  melting inside me (Ps 22:14).

As we pour out our feelings to God in all honesty,
we also need to listen. At first we may only hear our
own hollowness and emptiness and dryness. Maybe we
will feel swallowed up in our painful feelings and have
to move away from prayer and forget the process for a
while because it is just too much. But we need to keep
coming back. Gradually we will learn to hear God's
quiet, gentle, persistent, hopeful voice (cf 1 Kgs 19:
9-13). Many times a line from scripture can suddenly
become a powerful comfort or a guiding force for us.
At other times a flicker of insight or a long-needed sense
of hope or peace will come to visit us in a remembered
line from a letter of a friend, or in the sound of the
wind, or in the refrain from a song that echoes in our
soul. Perhaps quite imperceptibly the truth of the ages
about a God of love will come home to us. Slowly we
will catch glimmers of hope, of peace, of understanding, of acceptance.

We may often walk away from our prayer time wondering if it was worth it, or if God was really there
because we felt nothing or we felt only negative feelings. The secret is to be faithful to the quiet and the
solitude, to continue to cry out to God and to make the
attempt to be still in order to hear the truth. It is often
in our poverty of spirit and our helplessness that we
realize we cannot pray by our own efforts alone. It is
God who comes to pray in us in our dark and sad moments (Rom 8:26). We are there, awaiting the blessing
of hope. It is then that we understand the prayer of
Ephesians: ''Glory be to him whose power, working in

us, can do infinitely more than we can ask or imagine''
(Eph 3:20).

3. Ritualization

As we become reflective and ponder the pain of our
goodbye, we also need to ritualize it. Ritual includes two
elements: a) the use of images or symbols and b) the
use of some kind of *movement* in our prayer. With these
two elements we thus act out some of the pain in us.

I discovered the value of ritualization as I acted out
one of my own goodbyes. It was mid-November and I
was hurting from the loss of a significant job change.
After three months in my new ministry, I was still feeling the loneliness and vulnerability of a different place
and a separation from good friends. Even though it was
cold and windy, I went for a long walk. My heart felt
heavy and my mind was as grey as the weather. Then
I spied a milkweed plant along the roadside. I walked
over and looked at its almost-empty seed pods. I felt
bonded with them. They were being twirled away in the
wind, and I knew that wherever they landed they would
root and grow green there. I took one of the seed pods
home with me and as I walked along the seed pods
spoke to me of my need to let go, of the necessity of
my investment in the present. I kept the seed pod in my
office during the rest of that year and when the pain of
letting go pounded on my inner door, I would look at
the seed pod and gain strength from it. Every time I
did so, I felt the strength to accept the present moment.

The milkweed pod was a means of connecting my
prayer to my life experience. Ritual can do this for us.
It is our life that we bring with us into our goodbye
prayer. So we search for images or symbols that speak
to us deep down at the center of ourselves. Then we

take our images or symbols and create some gesture of expression, some significant movement, out of which comes a connection with God, our self, and our life.

There are many images and symbols in scripture which speak vividly of such things as loss, death, farewell, hope, strength, guidance, transition and transformation. The image of dry bones coming to life and dancing in the graveyard is a wonderful message of hope (Ez 37). The images of fullness and harvest in the book of Ruth follow images of great emptiness at the beginning of that story. The compassionate shepherd bandaging the wounds of the sheep is given as a sign of God's care in Ezechiel (Ez 34). The wilderness of Exodus can remind us of our own inner and outer times of struggle and tough journeying. Jesus uses flowers and birds to caution against useless worry and anxiety and a grain of wheat to speak of the transition that is possible only if one is willing to go through the dying part of life (Lk 12; Jn 12). These and many other images of scripture speak to inner recesses of our beings.

Many of the common things of our life are also waiting to speak to us of our pain and to connect us to the inner spaces where deeper meaning lies. There are innumerable ordinary images that can be used to call forth reflection on the hurt within us. Birds going south for another season can speak of the necessary transitions in life. Weeds pulled from the lawn or wastebaskets full of trash may remind us of the unwanted parts of our lives that we yearn to be rid of. Envelopes without letters, torn clothes or lost buttons, incomplete puzzles, empty anythings, all these can be signs of our being unfinished. Ashes in the fireplace, dying plants or autumn leaves, empty nests, all these can be dimensions of the dying that life asks of us. The harshness of life can be seen in images such as uprooted trees, pieces of glass or torn paper. Shoes or suitcases might be a means of calling us to ponder our own inner or outer roads of travel.

There are also many common objects in life that can speak of new life and future hellos. Many times I have placed an object before a group and have asked them to connect their inner life with the object and the theme of the presentation. I am always amazed at the variety of valuable connections that people make. I have also asked participants to find an object that was an image of the goodbye or loss which they were currently experiencing. Once a man in his 40s brought a small chain, wrapped it around his wrists and spoke of the chain as his struggle to break through his macho, unfeeling culture. A woman brought an empty nest before the group and spoke of her last child leaving home. A widow of just six months held up a butterfly sculpture and said that each time she looked at it, the silent message was that someday the pain of loss in her world would lessen. A young man struggling with how to use his gifts and talents shared how a little seed with a green shoot in it had been enough to encourage him to say yes to a new position which was scary and risky. The stories go on and on and so does the beauty found in images and their messages of healing.

Just as we can so easily take the use of images for granted, so too with the use of movement. In movement, we bring our bodies with us to prayer as we connect our hurt with the God of healing. It is the whole of our person which is at prayer. Movement or physical action helps us to put our whole self into the process. As with images, scripture mentions many movements which ritualize the experience of goodbye and transition. There is the walk of the two on the road to Emmaus when they encounter Jesus and tell him the story of their downcast faces. It was in the carrying of the Ark of the Covenant that the Exodus people made their way through fear, discouragement and resentment to the Promised Land. Healing came in the washing of the leper, Naaman, in the river. There is ritual movement in the touch of Jesus upon the sick and in the jumping and dancing of the cripple made well in the Acts of the Apostles. The walk of the woman to the well and the hurrying back to tell the people of her inner healing ritualized her farewell to a sinful life.

Our everyday movements can also speak to us on a deeper level if we open ourselves up to them. Some movements or physical gestures that can help us to act out our grief are:

- sharing a meal with a friend as a love-bond with someone who nourishes us in our emptiness
- emptying a seed pod and realizing that we, too, have to let go before new growth can come
- lighting a candle to dispel our inner darkness
- emptying and cleaning closets or boxes while we are ridding ourselves of some inner clutter
- looking at photo albums when we need to remember the love and joy that past journeys have offered to us
- writing a letter in a lonely time as a reminder of connections of love that we still have

Once I prayed the passion and death of Jesus by reflecting on the emotions of each event and I then used water colors to speak of the deep hurt that was there. As I painted the events, the colors cried out the pain to me and created an inner openness where I could connect some of my own pain with that of the Crucified One.

Another movement that is also a vital part of grieving
and praying a goodbye is that of touch. Jesus could so
easily have healed, and sometimes did, without the
touch of his hand. But so often he stretched out his hand
and the vibrancy of his being was power indeed for
those who needed healing. Not long ago, a father spoke
with me about the death of his son, aged 16. The father
said it had been two years and his heart still hurt deeply
whenever he remembered the tragic death. Yet, he said,
the death of his son gave him something he had never
had before: a recognition of how valuable the touch of
another is. He told me how he had always been very
withdrawn or reluctant when it came to touching others,
even his own family. When his son died and he felt the
handclasps, the hugs and embraces from so many who
cared and grieved with him, he realized for the first
time what a powerful comfort and bonding an embrace
can be.

We cannot pray the ache out of one another but we
can bless it with the touch of our hands, the gift of our
hug and our embrace. When we do this, we give the
ache in the other permission to go on its way. Touch
fills a person's being with the energy of bonding and
love. Without ever saying a word, the message is given:
"I care. I am here for you. Here is some strength of
mine to go on; here is some love to energize you now
when you need it so much." Touch connects one to
another in care, makes contact with heartache, centers
love, concentrates spiritual energies, warms the cold or
exhausted spirit. Touch can penetrate barriers of despair, anguish, hardness or bitterness. A kiss on the
cheek, a quiet embrace, arms linked or hands held are
powerful movements in our ritualization of goodbyes.
Let us not be afraid to risk this valuable aspect of praying our goodbyes.

4. Reorientation

Where does prayer enter into our use of these gestures and images? How does the God-connection happen? It happens in the midst of our reflection and our ritualizing. It is there that life is gradually reoriented or given a renewed direction and energy. God dwells within, at the center and the core of our beings. When we use images, they connect our outer world to this inner world of our self where the divine dwells. This meeting is often an unspoken one. We sense it, but we do not always intellectualize it or have words for it. We connect with God much like the two from Emmaus connected with Jesus when their heartache on the road met the image of bread blessed and broken:

> Now while he (Jesus) was with them at table, he took the bread and said the blessing; then he broke it and handed it to them. And their eyes were opened and they recognized him; but he had vanished from their sight. Then they said to each other, "Did not our hearts burn within us as he talked to us on the road and explained the scriptures to us?" (Lk 24:30-32).

As the two walked along and talked with Jesus they did not know they were being healed. It was in the breaking of the bread that reorientation took hold. "Their eyes were opened," i.e., they began to understand and to accept what their past experience meant to them. They regained the gift of hope and opened themselves to the healing which they needed.

When an empty seed pod calls to our heart: "Let go!" or when a newly formed bud on a plum tree reminds us of hope, we are touching the space of our life where God dwells. It is our own Emmaus moment. Words from our heart to God's may follow the connection, but the connection itself can be a profound expression of our relationship to God. We are being reoriented, drawn into healing in a quiet sort of way.

Reorientation is a necessary element in praying our loss because this is where connections are made between our pain and the God of healing. It is where we bring faith to our grief. When we find some significance through our reflection and ritual, it gives us courage to go on. Many times I have looked at an image or have taken on some movement of farewell and have been blessed with an insight or a sense of meaning that was not there before. It reoriented my life.

One early summer I was out in the garden busily hoeing out the weeds that had decided to take over the patch. I didn't realize it but the garden had become a place of comfort for me as I prepared myself to move on to another ministry. I was finding it hard to leave a job, which I had created and developed, and place it in the hands and heart of someone new. On one particular morning I had a profound insight that was the beginning of great freedom for me. I saw the garden as my ministry, where I had planted and sown, where things had begun to grow. I saw that just as I would not be around to harvest its fruitfulness, neither would I be there to harvest the fruits of the ministry which I had begun. I remembered the words of scripture: "Neither the planter nor the waterer matters: only God, who makes things grow" (1 Cor 3:7). It was such a simple insight but it was the beginning of a cure for my heartache. Every day that I went to the garden from then on became a movement of farewell for me and a deliberate act of giving myself to the letting go process which I very much needed.

Yet another time I was out in the country on an autumn evening, going to visit friends on a farm. It was soon after the death of a dear friend of mine and the pain of loss was still extremely intense. As I walked up the sidewalk in the dusk, I heard the sound of geese flying south. I paused to be still and to listen. The sound of their southern flight filled me with tears of recognition. At the same time the strong image of geese in transition brought a twinge of hope to my heart. "How much a part of life," I thought, "is this going-away thing. My friend's home is with you, God. I cannot keep wanting to have her here with me in the way she used to be." I walked to the door that night with my first real acceptance of my friend's death. The ache returned many times, but each time it did, I could recall the evening that I paused to pray goodbye as I heard the geese winging their way south.

One of the most poignant stories ever told to me was by a grandmother who related how her grandson had died of sudden infant death syndrome. She told how her daughter and husband and their two children have since gone each year to the grave of the baby. On the baby's first birthday, they went to the winter cemetery and the children wrote "Happy Birthday, James" in the unmarked snow. It was their message of love to their young brother who had died. It was their way of ritualizing some of the love and farewell that they continued to carry with them in their hearts.

God Meets Us at the Bend in the Road

Each of us needs to connect and to integrate our pain of goodbyes. If we enter the goodbye prayer of recognition, reflection and ritualization, the healing connections and reorientation can be there for us. The fragments of our lives will come together and life will begin to make sense again. Hope will return to our hearts. I believe this because I have known it myself and have known so many others who have experienced this reorientation. It has assured me that the God of healing is ever present with us and will never fail us. God, who is love and light, will be the illumination we need and will rekindle our hope as we meet that significant bend in our road of life. It is then that the images and words of Psalm 18 will take hold in our hearts and be the kindling for the future:

> *I love you, Yahweh, my strength . . .*
> *you, yourself, are my lamp,*
> *my God lights up my darkness (Ps 18:1,28).*

Questions for Reflection, Integration, Discussion

1. What prayer do you return to when times are tough? What is there about this particular prayer that draws you to pray it?

2. What image has most spoken to you about your experience of loss? How has it spoken to you?

3. Have you ever personally ritualized a goodbye experience? If yes, what were some of the characteristics of this and how did you feel about it?

4. What scripture passage would you choose to use for praying your own present goodbye experience?

   What is the message in it that leads you to this choice?

5. Name a goodbye that you are currently experiencing. Review the aspects of praying a goodbye. How would you pray this particular one? (How would you identify it, reflect upon it, ritualize it?)

CHAPTER SIX

✧

New Melodies Break Forth From the Heart

When old words die out on the
    tongue,
new melodies break forth from the
    heart;
and where the old tracks are lost,
new country is revealed with its
    wonders.

—Rabindranath Tagore

There are stories told about those who have "died" and come back to life. They are life-after-death stories about bodyspirit sorts of things that proclaim: "I who have died am alive again today" (e.e. cummings). There are stories of the human heart that ring out this same strong truth. There are people who felt that all the songs in their heart had died, that all the roads they knew were wiped out and they could go no farther. Then a kind of resurrection happened within them and they discovered "new melodies" and the wonder of "new roads."

The following was written in celebration of the resurrection of a good friend, one who had tasted such deep depression that the thought of suicide was one of the sweetest comforts to her mind for many months. Then one grey winter day, life paid a visit and the dank darkness of her despair turned over like fresh black earth under a spring plow.

It is the story
of how fresh, fine fruit grew on a barren tree,
of how moonlight stalked the darkness and devoured it,
of how winter snows were snatched by strong southern
*   winds,*
of how an empty, hollow heart grew rich with the
*   fullness of an unseen presence.*

It is the story of one
who learned the penetrating power of silence,
whose heart listened more deeply than the ears of flesh,
who savored the faithfulness of friends who stood by,
who fled down the dark alleyways of depression and
*   walked into the ripe rims of Easter lilies.*

The seed in black earth
is no mere comfort slogan to the bereaved.
It is fully the groan and agony of one falling
into the hell of nothingness.
It is wholly the pain of one crawling out of the pit,
*   hands and knees on sharp rocks, spewing the blood*
of an angry search amid the stench of memories.

Many see only what is before them, some see not even
*   that.*
But the one who has been in the harbor of despair
ponders and savors the delicate, first curl of the
*   greening*
leaf in a grateful way that no one else ever can.

The one who has howled in the far countries of
*   darkness*
lingers long with the faint traces of light in the
*   dawn.*
The one who has torn into her past, with the rage of the
*   wild,*
snatches the first jagged pieces of her life's puzzle
and she shouts out like one in a field full of treasures:
"I have found my Self! I, who have died, have come back
*   to life!"*

When we are in a grief process, the time comes for us in our goodbye experience to move on, to allow new melodies to break forth from our hearts. The time this takes is different for each person. What may take several years for one may take only a few months for another. We cannot compare because we are all such unique beings. But moving on must eventually be a part of our journey toward wholeness. Moving on is the time of coming back to life, of recovering our inner dynamism, enthusiasm and our desire to get on with the business of life. Moving on usually comes slowly. Days and months may go by, with a kind of plodding along, of just going on; some describe this time as existing or getting through, doing what you have to do. Occasionally, flickers of hope rush through our spirit like fireflies on a hushed summer's night. Briefly we feel good; we feel a bit of coming home to ourselves, and then the feeling is gone again. Slowly, though, we do come back to life; new country is revealed to us. A quiet resurrection happens in us. Finally, there arises in us the desire to move ahead. Life will never be as it once was because we are changed. The first green shoot has pushed its way through the dark soil.

The reality of moving on is this: We can never do so until we let go of whatever binds us to the past. If we have a heavy burden in our heart, it will drag behind us and create an ever-weary and ever-sad atmosphere in our spirit. If we have a memory that eats away at our integrity or an anger that gnaws at our peace, we will not move on in freedom. It will always be there to stir up negative feelings in us. If we have anything in us to which we hang on too tightly, anything that causes us distressful feelings, it will weaken our walking forward on the journey. It will sap our inner energy and mar our vision of where we are going and of how life is meant to be for us. We simply must come to a place in our lives where we agree to give up old securities which bind us, or painful memories which harm us, or dashed dreams which discourage us, or heartaching wounds which prevent us from discovering new dreams and from coming into fuller life.

I have learned about letting go, not just through books or ideas or from what others have told me about the need to do so, but from my own life experiences. I have discovered two very significant things: Letting go never seems to get easy, and growth will not happen unless I can really surrender. Sadly enough, I have to keep re-learning this because I like to hold on. Just when I think I have finally come to the full realization of how necessary it is to let go, I see that I am once again holding onto something too tightly and there I am again, not free to grow!

Oftentimes, when I have spoken about the need of letting go, I can see confusion and concern in the eyes of the people present. Questions are raised: Does this mean that I shouldn't care anymore? Should I stop praying for my daughter's marriage difficulties? Do I have to block out all the past from my memory of a loved one who's died? What happens to my own will and my responsibility if I let go? Am I supposed to be completely passive and allow others to harm me by their decisions?

To let go does not mean that we give up or that we do not care. Rather, it means that we choose to use our energies in another way, giving them another direction. Instead of concentrating on what has been hurtful, we look to what will be life-giving. We wish that life could have been otherwise or that things could be different. But it cannot be, so we accept that fact and move forward. We continue to care deeply but we also realize that we cannot change what is. All the struggling and grieving of our hearts will not bring back a loved one who has died, or erase a failure of ours, or keep a child from growing up or a parent from aging.

To let go does not mean that we ignore old ragged and torn feelings and memories, or that we fail to recall the loved ones whom we miss so much. When these memories knock at the door of our consciousness, we open the door to see who is there and we acknowledge them. But we do not invite them in to spend the entire day with us.

To let go is to allow something or someone to be left behind in such a way that we are free to continue toward new country that is waiting to be revealed to us. It is to gain the freedom to proceed or to continue, to put behind us whatever has the power over us to negatively influence our feelings, ideas, actions. Letting go is an *attitude* that grows within us. It is never complete until it is acted upon.

Why is this action so hard to do? Why do we hang on so tightly? Perhaps because we fear not being in control or we fear insecurity. It is natural to want the known, the safe, the serene and the secure in our lives. Few of us like the feeling of uneasiness or uncomfortableness that change and letting go usually bring. We would rather cling to the present pain, the deadness, or the lack of life, than face what is foreign and unknown, no matter how good it is for us.

There are many different ways and times when letting go needs to be a part of us. We may need to let go of any of the following:

A person: This letting go may come through the death of a loved one, the termination of a friendship, a child going off to school or a son or daughter marrying. Life will never be the same as it was before those events took place. As we let go, we cherish the good memories and set aside the bad ones.

Unmet expectations: These can be expectations of ourselves, of our parents or of children, of friends or co-workers, perhaps of our church or our government. It can be extremely painful to finally accept a parent as he or she is, to see their flaws and weaknesses and to love them in their incompleteness. When a child so dearly loved continually makes poor choices and develops attitudes foreign to a parent's values, it can be a harsh and dreadful experience for a parent to let go of the child they hoped for and to accept the child that they have.

Dreams and goals: Especially at mid-life, but at any adult transition time, we come to "truth times" when we see who we are and how we are. We can't be like someone else, or we won't be wealthy, or we will not be whatever it is that we thought we might be.

Old injuries of the heart: We all have them. They claim a lot of our energy at times. It may be the person who never liked us, or the one who destroyed us with jealousy or untruths, or the one who wiped us out with silence. It may be the relative who started the fight or the parent who abused us verbally or physically. We must also let go of our sinfulness. It is very hard to accept our own weaknesses or our failures and to trust in the mercy and forgiveness of God.

Old securities: It may mean letting go of the outer strongholds of the place where we have lived for a long time or our present job, our set of friends, our known skills. We must sometimes let go of our inner securities as well: the way we think or feel about things or about ourselves; even our image of God needs to change as we grow and develop.

Our riches: Good health is a treasure. Sometimes

we are forced to let go of it. Perhaps it is the natural aging process of more wrinkles and less energy that we need to accept, or the inability to see well or to drive a car. We may lose it by a disease that slowly claims our body or a car accident that maims us in some way. There are internal treasures of which we also need to let go: consolations in our prayer life when the inevitable darkness and emptiness of spiritual growth comes; the hollowness and lethargy of depression that may take over the spirit; the ennui of mid-life that parks itself in the soul and seems as if it will stay forever. There are also those times when we are called upon to let go of the riches of friends who are close by, when a job promotion takes us far away and time or travel prohibit those regular conversations and enjoyable sharings that we once knew and valued so much.

Taking Action

If we want to let go, we must first recognize what it is that needs letting go; then we need to accept the wisdom and the necessity of not clinging to it. Finally, we must gather up all the energy of our will that we possibly can and begin to take action—to actually leave the grief of our loss behind us. It is not easy to do this.

I have known numerous people who have let go and have come to the freedom to move on in their lives. One was a woman who always wanted her father to show love for her. He never did, not even on his deathbed when she expressed her love for him as he lay dying. All her life she rightly expected some sign of affection from this father who was verbally harsh and critical of her. After his death and after much grieving, she had to come to terms with how much power this man had over her life; even after his death she was still ruled by memories of his non-affection. Writing a letter of farewell to him began the process of truly letting go, and it eventually allowed her to express a truth she had never wanted to accept: "My father will never tell me that he loves me." Each time the memory of her father's lack of affection surfaced, she gently put it aside with "That's all over now." As she did this, her father had less and less power over her feelings and the sadness, guilt and distress that she felt so deeply were also being erased.

Another letting go: A young man came to see me one day who was having tremendous anxiety over a dispute with his manager at work, a conflict situation in which he was obviously not at fault. After some reflective sharing, he discovered that he had never let go of what seemed to him to be a great failure of his life in a previous job. He had chosen to move and to seek new employment rather than to work out the hassles and the friction in the situation. The dispute in his present work brought back all those memories and he feared that he would again leave his job. Once he recognized his strong hold on his old, painful memory, he began to be freed. He took an afternoon by himself, wrote a dialogue between himself and the person in his former job with whom he had the conflicts. He then went to scripture and put himself into some of the healing stories. Eventually he, too, was able to let go of the old memory and found that it no longer had the power to create fear and anxiety in him.

A woman for years had kept anger in her heart toward a relative who had been harsh and unfair with her. Each time she knew that the two of them might be at a family gathering she would begin to plan out avoidance procedures. She would become extremely worried about her physical appearance, how she ought to look and how she would respond to situations that might develop. One day her spiritual director said to her: "Why do you allow your anger toward that person to have so much power over you?" Together they began to look at what forgiveness meant and to see that she did not need to be controlled by that old hurt. Each time she found herself planning ahead on what to wear or what to say, she would check herself with, "I don't need to worry about that. I do not need that person's approval. No harm is coming to me." She, too, let go of the past and became a very peaceful person when she was around her "old enemy."

Surrender

Surrender walks hand in hand with letting go. To surrender is to give over to God, to give up our power over something that keeps us down or holds us back. When we surrender, we open ourselves up to the mystery of life, to the risks of the future, to the challenge of the unknown.

During our time of surrender, we especially need a personal relationship with a God whom we believe cares deeply for us. We need this because surrender demands that we trust God with our lives. We trust that we will not be harmed, that the letting go will be beneficial to our growth. How else can we take those giant, risky steps into unmarked territory? Surrender raises hard questions for us: Are we willing to trust God with our lives, our gifts, our treasures? Do we believe that we have the inner resiliency to place ourselves in the hands of the future which we cannot see or name? Are we able to say with Ignatius of Loyola, "Take, Lord, receive, all is yours now . . . give me only your love and your grace. These are enough for me"? Obviously a surrender of this depth requires a tremendous openness and trust of God with our lives. Few of us can pray this prayer with our entire beings, but all of us can pray it with at least a portion of our hearts.

For many of us it is scary to think of surrendering ourselves into the arms of God. "What might happen?" is the secret question that pummels our thoughts. We do not yet fully believe that God is always yes, *always* desiring our good and our happiness. We do not yet fully realize that God will be with us as a guiding power to love and to sustain us through whatever hardships and heartaches life may bring.

Surrender to God is a highly freeing event. It is like opening the lid of a jar and letting the butterfly wing away freely, or like a person paralyzed for years being able to run and jump and dance again. It is the freedom of a bound Lazarus coming forth from the tomb.

Part of what keeps surrender from happening in us is our desire to be in control of everyone and everything. We want to make sure that it happens our way and in our time. And we all know that life is simply not that way, no matter how hard we try to work it out in our own control system. Much wisdom is needed to know when to be in charge and when to acknowledge our powerlessness and our inability to control all the events of our lives. We cannot just sit back and let everything happen to us. On the other hand, we cannot ignore the fact that there are aspects of our lives that we must let go of in order for us to grow.

Thus, to surrender is to have a willingness to be in another's hands, especially in God's hands, to be open to surprises and gifts we never dreamed possible. It is to hand over some of our own strong will to want to control everything, to let go of our own intense desire to make sure we never get hurt again. To surrender is to live with a mind and heart that is open to the future and to trust that all shall be well. When we let go and when we surrender, we are most surely on the pathway to healing.

Nature As a Source of Healing

One morning when I was in Israel I thought of how old wounds of goodbye rise up to haunt us. We were at Megiddo and someone in the group had found pottery shards there—a little fragment of a handle, a small section with a design on it. They were reminders of a city long buried. I knew that shards came to the surface after a rain, particularly a hard rain. I thought of those old hurts in us, how they rise up like pottery shards from the earth to remind us of what is still there inside us. We are always in need of more healing.

Nature has been a wonderful source of healing for me. It is often through nature that I find the insight and the courage to let go, to surrender, to move on. The following are some insights that have blessed me with moments of healing when I was in desperate need of them:

Fireflies in the dusk: I was walking out a great loneliness in my life one night. As I moved along the wooded path, I saw a bright light in the distance. I quietly drew closer and saw that it was only one tiny firefly. It was just a small fragile frame that was giving forth such brightness! The lone firefly then joined the dance of a hundred fireflies as I walked in the late dusk. All across the vast meadow, far into the woods, their little lights danced and brought me a sense of bondedness. They were like a silent symphony, a gift to my lonely spirit. Like Christmas tree lights without the strings to mar their freedom, the fireflies held vigil with me. They danced for the earth, giving light to its darkness and I thought they danced for me, a pure and simple gift of beauty in the night.

In our darkest hour, it is often the smallest spark that brings us the gift of light, be it ever so frail a flicker. It is the moment of simple grace in a softly spoken word, a letter from a friend, an unexpected phone call, a warm touch from a loved one, or even a glance at the earth in its moment of hope. God has blessed our spirits with his own fireflies. They are small and fragile but they fly in our dark woods and their little beaming lights seem brilliant in our need.

Trees: Probably the most healing gifts of nature for me have been trees. I am rarely with trees for very long without a sense of blessedness or the truth of goodbye resting in my spirit. I once spent an autumn weekend with an oak tree. I watched the old oak with its wide-reaching arms give away his summer celebration. All night and all day the dead, brown leaves fluttered and flapped across the porch to the ground. Each little rap of wind tugged at the branches and lifted off another leaf. It seemed to me that the old oak tree stood ready and surrendered to the autumn event. I felt like an intruder on his farewell, seeing the wide open, stretched out limbs, the quiet, peaceful stance of his letting go. On that particular weekend the wisdom of surrender was rooted much more deeply in me.

The Flight of Geese: In the country place where I used to live I would often be awakened in the night by the sound of geese going south for the winter. It was a welcome sound that always left my heart feeling a bit sad and a bit glad. Geese speak to the part of me that knows transition and change are necessary, that leaving secure situations is an essential part of growth. When I hear flocks of geese call and see their patterned flight, they encourage me to allow myself to stretch and to grow. There is also a part of me that fills with nostalgia. My spirit cries out to them: "Friends!" The flight of geese helps me to recall all the blessings that change and transition have meant for my own growth and all the special people who have walked through my heart because I have moved on. The migration of geese, and all birds, deepens the belief in me to keep traveling the inner roads when I would rather not go.

Frost: One winter morning I awoke to see magnificent lines of frost stretching across my window panes. They seemed to rise with the sunshine and the bitter cold outside. They looked like little miracles that had been formed in the dark of night. I watched them in sheer amazement and marveled that such beautiful forms could be born during such a winter-cold night. Yet, as I pondered them I thought of how life is so like that. We live our long, worn days in the shadows, in what often feels like barren, cold winter, so unaware of the miracles that are being created in our spirits. It takes the sudden daylight, some unexpected surprise of life, to cause our gaze to look upon a simple, stunning growth that has happened quietly inside us. Like frost designs on a winter window, they bring us beyond life's fragmentation and remind us that we are not nearly as lost as we thought we were, that all the time we thought we were dead inside, beautiful things were being born in us.

Kinship

Another valuable bonding is that which I have named "kinship." Kinship is not just another word for friendship, community or kinfolk. It may be all of those things combined and yet none of those things alone. Kinship is a rich bondedness that calls forth to the deepest part of ourselves. It is a mutuality of understanding, a sense of belonging, a union of spirits, a loving appreciation and a deep communion which comes from having known experiences similar to the person with whom we are bonded.

Kinship confirms our own journey and gives hope to our struggles. It encourages us to "hang in there" when the going gets particularly difficult or overwhelming. Kinship nourishes us in our empty places and tells us that the dreams which we think we have lost have not died. When we experience kinship there is a mutuality of understanding on a mind and a heart level. Something deep inside us connects profoundly with something deep inside the other. It is like recognizing a part of ourselves that we thought no one knew or could understand in such an accepting and knowing way.

Empathy and compassion are also a part of kinship. We can feel with the other and the other can feel with us. No words need be spoken. The solidarity of spirit is a loving resonance that speaks for itself. A union of spirits develops when one feels a value or a truth connected with the other who seems to walk some of the same inner footsteps of our own story of life. It is as if the vision in our own being meets the vision in another and something in us lights up in recognition, knowing that it is heard and accepted.

Kinship is deep communion that carries strength across many miles. We may not see each other often but we know and believe in the bondedness that exists. We draw strength from just knowing that the other is there and that she or he understands, that we can draw energy from one another in our time of need and return it just as generously when the time is called forth.

One day while reflecting on the gospel scene of John 19:25-27, the truth about kinship in the midst of suffering came home to me. There beneath the cross of a dying Jesus were his dear ones caught up in the heartache of his pain: a mother hurting for her only son, a disciple grieving for his friend and teacher. There was a strong thread of bondedness among those wounded ones. In a great gift of kinship Jesus, even in his own agony, reached out and touched the hurt of others. He gave his mother to John and John to his mother, knowing it would comfort the ache in each one to have a home in the heart of the other. How deep their mutual love of Jesus was and what a bonding it must have been for them in their days of loss. A heavy hurt was experienced beneath that Good Friday cross, yet the kinship that was shared helped them to withstand the cruel edge of death. We, too, stand beneath so many crosses where we hurt with loved ones who suffer. When we do so, God reaches into our ache and comforts us by giving us to each other in kinship just as Jesus did with Mary and the disciple, John.

This is what kinship is about: the gift of one to the other. It may be the kinship of a good friend, a friend whose heart is our second home, or it may be the kinship which we have with others because of a mutual experience which newly bonds us together in time of need. There are numerous support groups whose members feel a certain kinship—groups of recovering alcoholics or other substance abuse persons, families of cancer patients or those with other illnesses, parents who have lost a child through death or disappearance, men and women who are divorced or widowed, and many other groups whose members establish a bonding because of the understanding that connects them in their struggle. There is a strength in support groups which comes from the recognition that one's own process is normal and natural. One can look around the group and see others who are also trying to put the pieces of their lives back together again.

Kinship is not always easy. As we walk with others who are working through a loss, we may get very tired or impatient with their seemingly slow progress. We may become irritated with their self-orientation or their constant heavy heartedness or their strong hold on anger or breaking into tears at the most unpredictable times. It may take real effort to keep standing by them, but how necessary it is to do so. We need to be faithful. This is the gospel love which gives without expecting in return. We also need to extend invitations to growth, but when these invitations are not accepted we need not feel rebuffed or rejected. These refusals are simply indications that the grieving one is not yet ready to move on. Someday the time will be ripe and we will rejoice at our friend's new beginning. How easy it is for us to forget how long it took to go through our own goodbye moments and how patiently others stood by us. Kinship is grounded in the truth expressed in 2 Corinthians 1:3-4:

> Blessed be the God and Father of our Lord Jesus Christ, a gentle Father and the God of all consolation, who comforts us in all our sorrows, so that we can offer others, in their sorrows, the consolation that we have received from God ourselves.

Kinship is much needed for the healing of our woundedness. Our healing will be blessed by the consolation of understood pain and by a bondedness that supports us at times when we feel that the parts of our life will never reassemble into a whole again.

Recovering Hope

Kinship encourages healing and with healing comes hope. When we are moving on from our painful good-byes we have much in common with the gospel stories of the resurrection. When Jesus was raised from the dead it was an event that seemed beyond the disciples' comprehension. The gospels tell us that they were "slow to believe" (Lk 24:25), that they doubted (Jn 20:25), that they " did not believe" the hope of new life that was being proclaimed (Mk 16:11-15). "The story seemed pure nonsense" to them (Lk 24:11). The disciples lived with incredulity and struggle before they finally accepted the truth that Jesus had been transformed. It was only after Pentecost that they fully understood, that they could look back on what had taken place and could feel within them a new surge of energy and vitality to walk into the future.

It is a natural piece of the inner process of healing that we come to the truth of our newness gradually, sometimes believing that we are on the mend and then getting discouraged or falling back into emptiness or desolation. But we do have our own pentecosts, those moments in life when we can look back and know that we have finally walked out of our goodbye. It no longer weighs us down all the time or constantly influences our thoughts and feelings. We feel a freshness about the days. We are glad to be alive. Deep within there is a tiny trickle of new life that doesn't stop flowing.

Love endures and goes on, in spite of all the feelings of grief inside us. Deep down we know that love can go with us beyond death of any kind, and we know, too, that time and the gift of God are wonderful healers of the heart. People who say that they won't love again, won't trust again, won't risk again, won't try again, are in the stage the disciples were in when they were overcome with the death of Jesus and walked dejected and downhearted, thinking their lives would never hold meaning and happiness again.

The human spirit is astounding in its resiliency and its ability to recover hope. That is what the resurrection proclaims: the possibility of transformation, the belief that we can be filled with new life, that the future will bless us.

This is what I shall tell my heart,
and so recover hope:
the favours of Yahweh are not all past,
God's kindnesses are not exhausted;
every morning they are renewed;
great is God's faithfulness (Lam 3:21-23).

Your sun will set no more
nor your moon wane,
but Yahweh will be your everlasting light
and your days of mourning will be ended (Is 60:20).

Those who went sowing in tears
now sing as they reap.
They who went away, went away weeping,
carrying the seed;
they come back, come back singing,
carrying their sheaves (Ps 126:5-6).

We need to carry these promises of new life with us in our hearts, especially when hope seems far from us.

Moving On

What can we do as we move on to new country, as we are recovering hope and awaiting the melodies of new life to sing in us? If we are attentive to the following, we will be opening ourselves to the gift of our own spirit's resurrection:

- Be aware of your feelings and listen to what your inner world is saying.
- Accept what cannot be changed, be willing to let go.
- Be good to yourself by gifting yourself each day with little gestures of kindness (a talk with a friend, a walk with nature, listening to music, going fishing or playing tennis . . .).
- Open yourself to people; try to give yourself to just one helping situation, to gradually move out of your self-orientation.
- Keep leaning on God even when God seems far away.
- Trust in the power of God to restore you to health, to recover from your goodbye. Believe that God is a great strength.
- Keep returning to the truths in scripture.

This book is about goodbyes and how they happen in our lives and about what happens to us because of them. It is also a book about hellos. The pattern is unending: hello-goodbye-hello. It tells us of the seasons of our human journey. It proclaims that we do not need to stay lost or dormant forever. The "homesick crane" in us does find joy in the journey. We do have periods in our lives when we wing our way with great energy and vibrancy. We do have seasons when we enjoy the delight and the adventure of life's travels, when we savor the taste of recovered hope and relish the vistas of new truths. There is new country waiting for us. There are new melodies that yearn to be sung in our spirits. We must believe this even on our most desolate of days. The season of springtime, of hello, awaits us all.

> *Somewhere within*
> *the seed has sprouted.*
> *I can feel its movement;*
> *I can sense its energy.*
>
> *Somewhere within*
> *the rainfall has reached.*
> *My desert is gone,*
> *my dryness has disappeared.*
>
> *Somewhere within*
> *I've been given life again.*
> *I can say goodbye to emptiness;*
> *I can say hello to fullness.*
>
> *Somewhere within*
> *my yearning has been met.*
> *The God of graciousness has graced,*
> *the God of tenderness has blessed.*
>
> *Somewhere within*
> *I feel at home again.*
> *I have enthusiasm;*
> *I want to dream.*
>
> *And so*
> *the circle of my life-journey*
> *has once more*
> *come into its season of spring.*

Questions for Reflection, Integration, Discussion

1. What is the most difficult aspect for you in letting go and moving on?

2. What does kinship mean to you? Have you known this experience? If yes, with whom have you felt kinship and what was this like for you?

3. What scripture passage most speaks to you about hope and hello?

4. Has there been a time in your life when you experienced a process of healing and of recovered hope? How did this happen?

5. As you look back over your reading of and reflection on this book what have been the most significant insights for you? How have these insights influenced the way you look at goodbyes and farewells?

Prayers for Those
Experiencing Goodbyes

Introduction

The prayers in this section are extensions of Chapter 5. They incorporate both images and movement focusing on many kinds of loss. These goodbye prayers can be turned to as various forms of loss are experienced in one's life. Most are for individual use, but any of the prayers could be adapted for group prayer.

These prayers are not meant to be the totality of praying a goodbye. It is not expected that all the hurt will go away once the prayer is completed. Rather, the prayers are bridges, enabling the pray-er to move the pain of goodbye to the spiritual realm. These prayers acknowledge the deep cutting truth of grief. They are meant to allow God's entrance into the inner rooms of our hurt and to move a bit further into the healing process. Praying some of the prayers may begin a healing process or continue it, or perhaps be one of the significant, final gestures of closure in the process of moving on.

Although writing is not always specifically suggested for the prayers, it may be very helpful for you to have a journal or a notebook. Before beginning your prayer time, reflect on the following questions and write whatever comes to mind:

- How am I feeling as I begin this prayer time?
- What am I desiring to have happen in this prayer time? (For example, draw some needed strength, deepen a sense of God's presence, develop further healing.)
- How do I feel about my relationship with God?

It may also be helpful to write after the prayer experience, noting feelings, insights and deepened awareness. You may wish to write a prayer as your closing.

As you begin your prayer time, first quiet your mind and your body. Become aware of how you are feeling physically. Take some deep breaths. Close your eyes. Just be still and rest in the arms of God for a few minutes.

Each of the prayers offers an image to use. Images are excellent tools to connect our outer world to our inner world. For some, this will be a very inviting experience. For others who find imaging very difficult, it may be a struggle. The images are only suggestions. Do not let them get in the way of your prayer if they seem binding or constricting. But do give them a try. You may be surprised at how helpful they are.

Usually several scripture passages are offered for reading and/or meditation so that options are available.

May these prayers be a source of strength and another step toward the hello which will come in its own time.

Prayer of One Seeking Shelter
in the Storms of Life

Image: a candle burning

Opening Prayer

> Say the word *God* and let it pervade you. . . .
> God's hands are around you; they shelter your
> life as a flame is sheltered in the storm.
>
> Caryll Houselander

Pause to image God's hands around you; say the word
God and let it fill your being with a sense of shelter and
comfort.

Reflection

> *I know from experience:*
> *standing deep within a linden tree*
> *in a pouring summer rain shower,*
> *one will not get wet.*
>
> *I know from experience:*
> *sitting very close under scrub oak*
> *in a mountain downpour,*
> *one will not get wet.*
>
> *I know from experience:*
> *when we draw very near to God's heart,*
> *when we stand deep within God's shelter,*
> *we will not be overcome*
> *with the drenching pain of life.*

Scripture

Then he (Jesus) got into the boat followed by his
disciples. Without warning a storm broke over the

lake, so violent that the waves were breaking right over the boat. But he was asleep. So they went to him and woke him saying, "Save us, Lord, we are going down!" And he said to them, "Why are you so frightened, you of little faith?" And with that he stood up and rebuked the winds and the sea; and all was calm again. The disciples were astounded and said, "Whatever kind of man is this? Even the winds and the sea obey him." (Mt 8:23-27).

Meditation

Place yourself in the situation of the storm at sea. You are in the boat with Jesus. You move out into the deep waters and gradually the sky darkens. The wind rises. The terror of the storm moves in with dark violence.

What are the sounds that you hear? What do you see as you look into the face of the storm? How do you feel as the storm grows in fierceness and as the boat rocks precariously with the force of the wind and the waves?

Image Jesus in your boat. See how deeply he sleeps as the storm continues to rage. How do you feel about Jesus being asleep during the distress which you are experiencing?

Go over to Jesus and awaken him. Speak to him. Tell him how you feel about the storm at sea. Then, tell him how you feel about the storm in your life now.

Listen to Jesus rebuke the wind and the waves. See him turn to you and place his hand on your heart as he tells the storm within you to be calm and to be still.

Invite Jesus to sit beside you. Notice the sky clearing to a deep blue and the sea growing calm. Experience the comfort and peace of the presence of Jesus beside you. As you do so, you may wish to repeat verse 12 of

Psalm 2, quietly, slowly, allowing your heart to be at peace in the shelter of God:

Happy are all who take shelter in God.

Closing Prayer

God of my life, I am lost at sea; the wild winds and pelting rain of my troubles are threatening to submerge me in their power. I am tossed to and fro by the struggles that come upon me every day. There is so little energy in me to go on. I do not know how much longer I can hold on to hope. In my distress I cry out: Are you asleep in my boat of life? Do you care that I am battling the storm with every breath that I take?

Then your grace sweeps through my being and I remember the sacred voice of the ages:

> *If I flew to the point of sunrise,*
> *or westward across the sea,*
> *your hand would still be guiding me,*
> *your right hand holding me (Ps 139:9-10).*

All the truth of your sheltering love comes to comfort me in bits and pieces of the psalms: You do shelter me under your awning in times of trouble; you will hide me deep in the dwelling of your heart and protect me (cf. Ps 27:5). I know your love for me has been deep and strong since the moment of my conception for

> *you drew me out of my mother's womb;*
> *you entrusted me to my mother's breasts,*
> *placed on your lap from my birth,*
> *from my mother's womb you have been my God*
> *(Ps 22:9-10).*

So I beg of you, Comforting One who goes with me in the storm, look after me, I take shelter in you. Guard me like the pupil of your eye; hide me in the shadow of your wings, for I belong to you. I seek shelter, for you are my hope; you have always been my strength. I will rest in you, God, and trust that you will be with me no matter how great or how long or how intense this storm is. You are the source of my hope; with you for my strong support, my safety, I will make it through all this. Your arms are around me. They shelter me just as the flame of this candle before me is sheltered from the wind and keeps burning brightly. I entrust my life to you. Amen.

Prayer of One Who Feels Broken Apart

Image: broken pieces of a glass jar or paper torn into pieces

The following verses of scripture are often used to portray the tremendous suffering and brokenness of Jesus on Calvary. They can also be the image of those who have experienced their world as shattered, their once whole, peaceful lives strewn in pain. It is the image of those who feel their life can never be put back together again. If you are one of these brokenhearted ones, this could be your cry:

For all my foes I am an object of reproach,
a laughingstock to my neighbors,
and a dread to my friends;
they who see me abroad flee from me.
I am forgotten like the unremembered dead;
I am like a dish that is broken (Ps 31:12-13, NAB).

Prayer

Part of the beginning of your prayer time is either to
take a whole piece of paper and tear it into shreds or to
break a glass jar into pieces. In doing this you are ac-
knowledging the pain and the harshness which you feel
in your brokenness and which you are crying out to God
in your hurt. After the breaking of glass or tearing of
paper, the following reflection could be read.

Reflection

> *Jesus, your brokenness was real.*
> *All the joy of being alive*
> *all the beauty you saw in earthen things*
> *all the people you knew and loved*
> *all the satisfaction of healing*
> *all the blessedness of your teachings*
> *all the love you knew and shared*
> *all of this—shattered on that hillside.*
> *You were torn apart, broken, smashed.*
> *All of life's joy seemingly destroyed,*
> *terrible pain stretching out your agony.*
> *Only a handful beneath your cross*
> *to remind you of your wholeness,*
> *and even this handful of loved ones*
> *could not take your brokenness away.*
> *You were a broken piece of pottery,*
> *dashed against the stones of life,*
> *a thing to be thrown away,*
> *your flesh a ghastly thing to see,*
> *your aching spirit a painful knowing.*
> *On the cross that Calvary day*
> *the sacred unity seemed torn apart.*
> *Like a broken dish, like a broken dish,*
> *you went to your grave.*

Prayer

Image your life as a pottery jar. See your life broken apart. Look at all the pieces, harsh and jagged. Feel the brokenness that is yours. Now gather the pieces together. See yourself taking them to Jesus. Have him hold the pieces in his hands. Listen to him tell you about his brokenness, how the Father raised him from the dead and brought him to a wonderful wholeness. See the pieces of pottery in Jesus' hands come together into a beautiful jar. Take time to just look at the beauty of the jar. Then open your hands and receive the jar in its wholeness from Jesus. Pray your response.

Closing Prayer

Jesus, you were once broken apart. You know how it feels to be so shattered by the goodbyes of life. Help me to believe that I will one day experience wholeness again, that I will not have this terrible feeling of being torn into many pieces. Keep reminding me often that the Father raised you to new life, to a powerful wholeness that you had not known before. Encourage me to believe that, in time, I will no longer have this deep pain and hurt in my heart. I want to believe. Help my unbelief! Amen.

Prayer of a Pilgrim
Who Struggles With the Journey

Image: shoes

Take a pair of shoes that you wear a lot and place them in front of you as you pray this prayer. Let your shoes remind you of your constant movement, both on the outside and on the inside of yourself.

Prayer

Pilgrim God, there is an exodus going on in my life—desert stretches, a vast land of questions. Inside my heart your promises tumble and turn. No pillar of cloud by day or fire by night that I can see. My heart hurts at leaving loved ones and so much of the security I have known. I try to give in to the stretching and the pain. It is hard, God, and I want to be settled, secure, safe and sure. And here I am feeling so full of pilgrim's fear and anxiety.

O God of the journey, lift me up, press me against your cheek. Let your great love hold me and create a deep trust in me. Then set me down, God of the journey; take my hand in yours, and guide me ever so gently across the new territory of my life.

Walking Meditation

Take these words with you and go for a walk, preferably a walk where you can be alone with the scripture and can let the words of God to Jacob settle in your pilgrim heart:

Be sure that I am with you; I will keep you safe wherever you go (Gn 28:15).

Listen to the words of God to Jeremiah, also, as you walk along:

I know the plans I have in mind for you—it is Yahweh who speaks—plans for peace, not disaster, reserving a future full of hope for you (Jer 29:11).

After the Walking Meditation

Return to your place of prayer. Write down any thoughts, ideas, feelings which occurred to you as you walked your pilgrim prayer.

To close your prayer time, you might choose to do one or more of the following:

> Write your own prayer.
> Pray the pilgrim prayer that follows.
> Listen to the song "Journeys Ended, Journeys Begun" by the Weston Priory Monks (on the album: *Spirit Alive*).
> Pray Psalm 125.

Pilgrim Prayer

God of my life, create in me the heart of a pilgrim. There is a part of me that fights letting go. Do not allow me to become so rooted or so accustomed to my daily tasks and inner securities, that I miss your voice calling me to greater growth and deeper maturity in faith. I want to hoard my blessings, to hang onto my gifts, to hide my talents and the blessings of my life. I want to take them out, one by one, only when I know that it is safe and I won't get hurt or emptied. Stir afire in me such a great love for you and your people that I will constantly celebrate life and appreciate its beauty, even when it is painful. Allow me to "see visions and dream dreams" so that I can live with your vision and not be overwhelmed by the struggles of the journey. God of the Exodus, I know you are near. Grant me the courage to change, whether that change is an inner or an outer one. Deepen my awareness of your faithful presence and bless my pilgrim heart. Amen.

Prayer For a Lonely Day

Image: anything that is incomplete (For example: a shoe without a shoestring, an envelope with an address and no stamp, a blouse without a button, a cup with nothing in it.)

As you begin your prayer, look at the incomplete object. Let it be a sign of how you feel in your loneliness: incomplete, needy, empty, longing for a sense of wholeness in the love of another. You may want to write down your feelings as you look at the object. Continue your prayer time by reading the scripture passages below very slowly and reflectively. Choose one of the three passages and take some time to let the lines and words soak into your lonely spirit.

Scripture

> Father of orphans, defender of widows,
> such is God in his holy dwelling;
> God gives the lonely a permanent home
> (Ps 68:5-6).

> Listen, the time will come, in fact it has already come, when you will be scattered, each going his own way and leaving me alone. Yet I am not alone, because the Father is with me. I have told you all this so that you may find peace in me. In the world you will have trouble, but be brave; I have conquered the world (Jn 16:32-33).

> Then Jesus came with them to a small estate called Gethsemane, and he said to his disciples, "Stay here while I go over there to pray." He took Peter and the two sons of Zebedee with him. And sadness came over him, and great distress. Then he said to them, "My soul is sorrowful to the point of death.

Wait here and keep awake with me." And going on a little further he fell on his face and prayed. "My father," he said, "if it is possible, let this cup pass me by. Nevertheless, let it be as you, not I, would have it." He came back to the disciples and found them sleeping, and he said to Peter, "So you had not the strength to keep awake with me one hour?" (Mt 26:36-41).

Listen to the song: "Jesus the Lord" Roc O'Connor, S.J. (*Lord of Light* album)

Unite with Jesus in his loneliness in the Garden. Place yourself there with him. Ask him to tell you about his loneliness. Be still and listen. Then speak to Jesus about your loneliness. Tell him what it feels like. Invite him to be with you in your lonely moments.

Unite with all the lonely ones of the world. Ask God to bring a gentle presence of love and companionship to the following:

- those who have recently experienced the death of a loved one
- those who do not believe that anyone loves them or that they are loveable
- the orphaned, homeless, widows and widowers, the aged and those who lie in loneliness in hospitals throughout the world
- those who cannot sleep at night, who lie awake for hours in their loneliness, fears, anxieties or sadness
- those who feel that they stand alone in misunderstanding, rejection, abandonment or betrayal
- those who feel alone in their dreams of a world at peace and a world alive with gospel values

Closing Prayer

Thank you, God of the lonely, for the call to wrestle with loneliness. Help me to not run from it or to give in to it by buying things, withdrawing from others or compensating by eating or drinking too much. I pray that I can be with this feeling of ache and longing for companionship and happiness. God, you have said that you will give the lonely a home. Well, I need a home so much now, a sense of belonging and of being loved, of having a home in the heart of another. Please help me to be aware of how much you love me and how strongly you are a companion to me at all times. Come, visit me with your peace and your love. Come, make your home in me and I will make mine in you. Help me to reach out to others and to go forth from here with hope in my heart.

Prayer to Regain One's Inner Strength

Image: the eagle

The scriptural image of the eagle pictures it as the symbol of strength and long life, a sign of blessing; the eagle is also seen as an image of God, carrying us, holding us up, protecting us like a young one is protected in the nest.

Picture yourself as the young eagle, helpless, needing to be fed, learning to fly. See how the parent eagle holds you up, encourages you, protects you. Then image yourself as an adult eagle with strong wings, flying in the sky.

Reading

Where do you get the strength to go on when you have used up all of your own strength? Where do you turn for patience when you have run out of patience, when you have been more patient for more years than anyone should be asked to be, and the end is nowhere in sight? I believe that God gives us strength and patience and hope, renewing our spiritual resources when they run dry (*When Bad Things Happen to Good People*, Harold S. Kushner).

Scripture Verses for Prayer

Phil 4:13   *There is nothing I cannot master with the help of the One who gives me strength.*

Is 40:31   *Those who hope in Yahweh renew their strength.*
They put out wings like eagles.
They run and do not grow weary,
walk and never tire.

Ex 19:4   *You yourselves have seen how I carried you on eagle's wings and brought you to myself.*

Dt 32:11   *Like an eagle watching its nest,*
hovering over its young,
he spreads out his wings to hold him,
he supports him on his pinions.

Prayer of Acceptance

Stand with arms widely outstretched on either side, in the fashion of eagles' wings. Lift up your head and receive the strength of God. Let it flow through you. Then let your arms fall at your side, take a comfortable position of standing, sitting or kneeling. Pray the following prayer:

God of strength, who calls forth eagles to bend wings in adoration, who sends forth eagles to wing wide in praise, I am in need of your strength. I am weary, tired, unable to soar in my sky of life. Carry me on your loving wings. Renew my strength. Give me the energy for the going and create in me an openness to future flying. Great God of eagles' hearts, I want to trust that you will bear me up, that you will support me. I look to you to renew my strength just as surely as eagles' wings are wide in the sky. Amen.

Listen to the song: "On Eagle's Wings" by Michael Joncas (*On Eagle's Wings* album).

Prayer of Farewell to One Who Is Leaving

Image: the circle of loved ones, a sign of love unending

   Gather as a group, form a circle with your chairs.

Leader: Let us sit in silence for a few minutes, remembering the presence of our God who is with us and who understands the goodbye we are experiencing.
Prayer by leader: (after some minutes of silence) God of our life's journeys, we gather here to celebrate the goodness of _____ and to ask your blessing as he (she) continues on the road of life. May the love that is in our hearts be a bond that unites us forever, wherever we may be. May the power of your presence bless this moment of our leave-taking.

Listen to (or sing) the song: "When Someone We Love" (Weston Priory, *Rise Up* album):

   When someone we love so carefully grows
   With courage and struggle to let love be their
   home.
   We sing, yes, we dance and share our delight

*To witness such beauty and a strength, oh, so
right.*

*We love you dear friend, and we treasure your life.
We tenderly hold you in the palm of our hands.*

*The joy that you've found is gift for us all,
It glows like the velvet of a crystal moonlight.
Over the years the choices you've made
Have clothed you with freedom to nurture, to heal.*

*We love you dear friend, and we treasure your life.
We tenderly hold you in the palm of our hands.*

*And as we move on to horizons of light,
We hope for each other, drink deeply of life,
To know and to love, to choose and to share
This is the garden where happiness dwells.*

*We love you dear friend, and we treasure your life.
We tenderly hold you in the palm of our hands.*

Scripture: Acts 20:1-6, 36-38

Pause for reflection (Remembering the good qualities of
the one who is leaving.)

Response: Each of the group then thanks the one who
is leaving by naming one or more of the good qualities
of that person. For example: ''Thank you _____, for
being such a good listener.'' ''Thank you, _____,
for your sense of humor.'' ''Thank you, _____, for
the gift of your generosity.''

Closing Prayer: (all make response after each Leader statement.)

Response: We know that God goes with you.

Leader: As you journey onward, may you remember
always that our love and appreciation for you are etched
on our hearts . . .

Leader: As you experience the pain of change and the insecurity of moving on, may you also experience the blessing of inner growth . . .

Leader: As you meet the poor, the pained, the stranger on your way, may you see in each one the face of our Christ . . .

Leader: As you walk through the good times and the hard times, may you never lose sight of the shelter of God's loving arms . . .

Leader: As you question your decisions and wonder about the fruits of your choices, may the peace of God reign in your heart . . .

Leader: We praise and thank you, God of the journey, for our loved one who is soon to leave. We entrust _____ into your loving care, knowing that you are always the Faithful Traveler and Companion on our way. Shelter this loved one of ours and protect him (her) from all harm and all useless anxiety. May the future be a source of many enriching and transforming moments. Amen.

The leader then invites the group to join hands and to pray the Our Father.

The prayer closes with each one making the sign of the cross on the forehead of the one leaving as a sign of God's blessing and protection in the days to come.

Prayer of One
Who Has Been Betrayed By Another

Image: spittle on the face of Jesus

Find a quiet place where you can be alone. Begin by recalling the presence of God within you; feel the strength of God's love move through your being; image God's hand in yours as you begin to tell the story of your hurt to him. Review the situation(s) of rejection and pour out your heart with all its thoughts and feelings to God who is listening very attentively to you.

Read and meditate

Mt 26:67 *Then they spat in his face and hit him with their fists.*
Mt 27:30 *And they spat on him and took a reed and struck him on the head with it.*
Wis 2:19 *Let us test him with cruelty and with torture and thus explore this gentleness of his and put his endurance to the proof.*
Is 50:6   *I offered my back to those who struck me, my cheeks to those who tore at my beard; I did not cover my face against insult and spittle.*
Mt 26:23 *Someone who has dipped his hand in the dish with me will betray me.*

Reflection

> *Jesus, I come to you,*
> *overcome with revulsion*
> *by the spittle on your face.*
> *it slides down your cheeks,*
> *it comes in the corner of your eye,*
> *it sickens me, that sight.*
>
> *I cry out in that ugliness.*
> *I come to you, Jesus,*
> *with cloth and water*
> *to wipe away degradation,*
> *to wash away the filth,*
> *thrown from the bystanders.*
>
> *You lower your head to my hand*
> *and the slime comes on the cloth,*

it hardly washes in water
so thick is it upon your face.
the touch of human defilement
clings to the creases of your cheek.

I have felt this painful deed
as I, too, have known rejection,
have heard, and hurt, with words,
thrown like spittle in my face.

I have felt marred and maimed in spirit
as my very person was cruelly rebuffed.
I have felt the slime and contempt
stick and press upon my life, too.

The recognition of my own pain and derision
almost overpowers my sad soul;
I stand stunned and sorrowful inside myself.
I want to comfort you, Jesus;
I want to be comforted by you;

Jesus, spat upon and rejected,
have mercy on us all.

Imaging Prayer

Look at Jesus as he is spat upon and hit by others
and called names and jeered with cruelty; hear, see,
feel this rejection. See yourself in the place of Jesus;
hear, see, feel the rejection. Look at Jesus reach out to
comfort you. He wipes the spittle from your face as you
wipe it away from his cheek. He looks at you with great
love and deep understanding.

Prayer to believe in your self-worth again and to open
yourself to the possibility of loving and being loved:

Keep my heart open to loving others and to being
loved by them, God. Do not allow me to close off my

life because of the scars of this painful rejection. Lead me into peace of heart. Help me to believe in my own goodness, so much so that I can reach out to others with confidence and receive their affection with trust. I pray for all those who have been brutally and harshly betrayed . . . and I pray for the one who has rejected me. Jesus, you continued to be a loving person even though you had been so painfully treated. Please help me to be a loving person, too. Amen.

Closing: You may wish to pray your own prayer or listen to the song: "With What Great Love" by Carey Landry (*Abba Father* album).

Prayer of One Who Is in Constant Physical Pain

Image: your hand touching the hem of the robe of Jesus

Begin your prayer time by reflecting upon your illness; be aware of your feelings, both of body and of spirit.

Opening Prayer

God of oneness, wholeness, I hurt and pain and I dream of a day when I no longer feel continual distress in my body. I cry out to you to hear me, to stretch your arms of compassion to me and to embrace me with your comfort. My being needs to be filled with your spiritual energy. I am weary with the struggle to feel well and to be in good health. It is so easy to slide into depression and self-pity, to be impatient and despondent. God of the living, hear me. Fill my empty places with hope.

Fill my life with a sense of joy in spite of this ceaseless pain. Help me to fight that giant oppressor of the spirit: discouragement. Remind me often of the good people of my life and of all the blessings that are mine as I struggle with this pain which is ever present to me. I praise and thank you for being a God who never leaves me.

Reflection

Read Lk 8:40-48, the story of the woman who had been ill for 12 years.

Picture yourself in the crowd. See Jesus there. See what a loving, kind person he is. Feel a drawing to him in your heart. Image yourself going to Jesus, leaning down, touching the hem of his garment. Feel the tremendous spiritual power that moves from Jesus into your whole body and soul. Hear Jesus ask: "Who touched me?" See yourself stand up and speak to Jesus. Speak whatever comes to your mind and heart. Then listen to what Jesus speaks to you. Perhaps he will tell you that you are being healed or that your pain can be a source of inner transformation, or maybe Jesus will tell you how you are to live with your pain. Perhaps he will speak no words to you at all, only look on you with a deep compassion and understanding.

Pray your response to Jesus.

Closing Prayer (Ps 18—adapted)

I love you, God. I know you are my inner strength, especially now when my body does not have the strength that I took for granted in the past. God, my deliverer, I turn to you. Sometimes I feel that I do not want to go on. I get swallowed up by the floods of self-pity and discouragement. In my distress I cry out to you. Reach out to me and rescue me from the enemy of pain. Set me free of its grasp of resentment. Fill me with courage. When the darkness of constant pain threatens to overcome me, brighten the darkness with your presence. With you by my side I can go through this. You are like a rock. You will be my strength. You are like a shield. You can protect my spirit from being broken by my body's pain. I will keep coming to you, touching the hem of your garment of love and feeling the spiritual energy which you share with me. I love you and I place my trust in you. Amen.

Prayer of One Who Feels Lost

Image: a map

Begin your prayer by holding the map in your hand. Let it be the expression of the lost-ness that you feel within yourself.

Reflection

"You know the way to the place where I am going." (Jn 14:4).

> *Do I know, Jesus?*
> *I feel very lost.*
> *Are you my guide,*
> *the shepherd always there?*
> *How do I know the way*
> *when I've never been there?*
>
> *Is it that you are with me,*
> *that you make the way known*
> *in the tiny whispers of life,*

footstep by footstep,
bit by bit,
on the long journey of life?

Pray *Ps 107*
Read *Ex 13:17-22*

Prayer

God of Exodus, I am off on an inner road never traveled before. Deep within, where only your eyes see, there is so much mystery, greyness, restlessness. I want so much to have a sense of direction, to know where I am and where I ought to be headed. But the dark and the questions stay. You ask me to be full of faith, to believe deep within that you are my signpost, that you are my wisdom and my guide, and to trust in your presence. Your words to me are clear: "Do not fear. I go before you."

But the winter of my spirit wears on. The days pass by. I plod along like boots too big on a small child. Only, I do not marvel like the young one, or pause to wonder at the beauty. Instead, I just trudge and forge ahead, no spark of love, no charge of joy, no spiritual energy. Just a dead walk through an aimless winter. Everywhere in me I cry out for you, God; I yearn for you. I desire you greatly. And every now and then you come to me, sear my soul, wash over my thirst, soften my edges, glimmer in my darkness. So I know all is not lost. I am not lost, at least not forever. God of my depths, I cry out to you to be my guide. Help me to have a strong sense of inner direction and grant that I may have the reassurance of knowing that I am on the right path. Take all that is lost in me and bring it home to you.

Reflection

Bring your feeling of disorientation and lack of direction to God. Place all these feelings in God's hand. Trust God to walk with you and to give you an inner direction. Quietly repeat the following prayer several times, until it seeps into your soul. Breathe slowly. Be still. Trust.

Prayer: Show me the way in which I should walk.
For to you, O God, I lift up my soul (Ps 25).

Closing prayer

> *Dear God,*
> *why do I keep fighting you off?*
> *One part of me wants you desperately,*
> *another part of me unknowingly*
> *pushes you back and runs away.*
>
> *What is there in me that*
> *so contradicts my desire for you?*
> *These transition days, these passage ways,*
> *are calling me to let go of old securities,*
> *to give myself over into your hands.*
>
> *Like Jesus who struggled with the pain*
> *I, too, fight the "let it all be done."*
> *Loneliness, lostness, non-belonging,*
> *all these hurts strike out at me,*
> *leaving me pained with this present goodbye.*
>
> *I want to be more but I fight the growing.*
> *I want to be new but I hang onto the old.*
> *I want to live but I won't face the dying.*
> *I want to be whole but I cannot bear*
> *to gather up the pieces into one.*
>
> *Is it that I refuse to be out of control,*
> *to let the tears take their humbling journey,*

to allow my spirit to feel its depression,
to stay with the insecurity of "no home"?

Now is the time. You call to me,
begging me to let you have my life,
inviting me to taste the darkness
so I can be filled with the light,
allowing me to lose my direction
so that I will find my way home to you.

Prayer of One Experiencing Adult Transition

Image: anything with your name on it (driver's license, credit card, an envelope, etc.)

Begin by looking at your name, the letters, the words, which identify you. Close your eyes and look lovingly upon yourself. Contemplate the wonder, the joy, of who you are.

Reflective reading: "firefly"

my life. 40.
bend in the road.
I'm taking it.
need to.
where? don't know.
anxiety.
what's ahead?
I love to look back.
beautiful.
friends. success.
security.
ahead?
who knows?
looks dark.

beckoning.
saying: it's time.
it's time.
are you my firefly, God?
the flickering light
in the darkness?
are you on the road
around the bend?
do you nudge and urge me
to move on, to not nest,
to risk, to let go?
O God, loving God,
to whom I most belong,
be that darting firefly

but a glimmer of light
like a firefly
darts here and there.
calling to me.
encouraging my heart.

on the road.
catch my attention.
fix my heart's gaze
on you again
and on the wonder of life.

Read and Pray: Ps 139

Meditation

Gently move through your life. Note the times you have grown, when you have discovered something more about who you are and what life means to you. Take time to feel the pain of those discoveries and the gradual peace and joy that evolved as you had some distance from those events and situations. Open your hands as a gesture of surrender to God in this present moment of your transformation. Pray a prayer of trust to God and sit in silence with the One who promises to be with you in this time of transition.

Prayer

O Lord of revelation, once again I find myself opening up to another life process, full of pain, full of mystery and a certain aching wonder. I hear you calling me to face new beginnings, to leave the old behind, to discover new and deeper parts of my total being. O Lord God, help me to realize that I can be free, that I am being freed at this present moment. Let me look beyond my own small world and smile on the mysterious way that you allow each one of us to grow into the best of our own uniqueness. I want to live and to love the mystery. I remember the wonder and newness of discovering myself as person. I recall how I began to respect and to love the secret of who I am, of how I began to sense the greater and fuller dimensions of becoming "me." I thank you for all the tastes you have given to me of myself through the crises of my life.

O God of revelation, I offer you the struggle and the beauty of being human. I ask your blessing as my human growth continues to be revealed in the midst of my daily activities. I realize that my birth was just a beginning, just a first step in the continuous series of births that have called me to constant dyings and risings, to a deeper and more meaningful life. I hear now another call to die and to live more deeply, to live more wholly, more fully, a call to be opened and freed. Of God, it takes so much time to bring all of myself to birth—a lifetime—and I become so impatient. This anxiousness and this anxiety I feel . . . it's healthy, you say? It's all right? It's a part of my existence? It's shaping my heart into yours? Fully human? Ah yes, my God, let me not fear the mistakes or the failures or the anxieties that come with growth; rather, let me see in all of this process the signs and the strength of your cross and your resurrection. Let me know the blessing of your presence in this ever-birthing life of mine. Amen.

Prayer of One Who Is Moving On

Image: a suitcase

(Place your suitcase in a position where you can see it during this prayer time.)

Read and Pray: Ps 121

> *Yahweh guards you from harm,*
> *he guards your lives.*
> *He guards your leaving, coming back,*
> *now and for always (Ps 121:7,8).*

Prayer

Guardian, guide, no pillar of cloud by day nor fire by
  night,
Yet I sense your presence with me, God of the journey.
You are walking with me into a new land.
You are guarding me in my vulnerable moment.
You are dwelling within me as I depart from here.
You are promising to be my peace as I face the struggles
of distance from friends and security,
the planting of feet and heart in a strange place.

Renew in me a deep trust in you. Calm my anxiousness
As I reflect on my life I can clearly see
how you have been there in all of my leavings,
You have been there in all of my comings.
You will always be with me in everything.
I do not know how I am being resettled,
but I place my life into the welcoming arms of your love.

Encircle my heart with your peace.
May your powerful presence run like a strong thread
through the fibers of my being. Amen.

Suitcase reflection

- What blessings of your life do you most want to carry
  with you as you move on? Name these. (You may
  wish to write them.) Thank God for the gift to carry
  these blessings with you in your heart as you move
  on.
- What blessings are you most in need of as you continue your journey? Name these. (You may wish to

write them.) Pray for the grace to have these as a part of your journey.

- If you wrote your blessings on paper, place these lists in your suitcase as a prayerful sign of your trust in God.

Closing Prayer

(This litany is based on the four aspects of prayer: praise, thanksgiving, sorrow, petition.)

I give you praise, God of my journey,
for the power of love, the discovery of friends, the truth of beauty
for the wonder of growth, the kindling of fidelity, the taste of transformation
for the miracle of life, the seed of my soul, the gift of becoming
for the taste of the little dyings which have strengthened me for this moment
for the mystery of journey, the bends in the road, the pauses that refresh
for the faith that lies deep enough to permeate discouragement and anxiety

I give you thanks, God of my journey,
for all I have learned from the life of Jesus of how to say goodbye
for those who have always stood near me and given me spiritual energy
for your strength on which I can lean and your grace by which I can grow
for the desire to continue on, for believing that your power works through me
for being able to love so deeply, so tenderly, so truly
for feeling my poorness, my emptiness, my powerlessness
for believing that you will care for me in my vulnerability

I ask forgiveness, God of my journey,
for holding on too tightly
for refusing to be open to new life

for fighting off the dying that's essential for growing
for insisting that I must be secure and serene
for ignoring your voice when you urged me to let go
for taking in all the goodness but being reluctant to share
  it
for doubting my inner beauty
for resisting the truth of my journey home to you

I beg assistance, God of my journey,
to accept that all of life is only on loan to me
to believe beyond this moment
to accept your courage when mine fails
to recognize the pilgrim part of my heart
to hold all of life in open hands
to treasure all that is gift and blessing
to look at the painful parts of my life and to grow through
  them
to allow your love to embrace me on the empty and lonely
  days
to receive the truth of your presence
to trust in the place of "forever hello"

Prayer of One Terminating a Relationship

Image: a closed door

Sometimes we need to break a relationship, to bid someone or something farewell. It may be a marriage that has died, a friendship that is no longer healthy, a job that has failed, an old memory that has haunted us long enough, etc.

Ritual of Termination

Find a private room in your home. Close the door tightly. Sit in front of the door, facing its closedness. Reflect on the person, or the job, or the situation, or the memory or feeling that you need to bid farewell.

Pray: Ps 143 (adapted)
I sit here before this closed door
and beg of you to hear my prayer.
Hearken to my pleading, faithful God.
You know how I have felt crushed,
hounded by this situation (or person)
and how the old memories pursue me
like an enemy in the dark.

Lead me forth from the prison of my past.
It is time for me to let go,
to bid farewell, to walk away.
I feel as if I have been dwelling in the dark
for so long, like someone long ago dead and buried.

Hasten to help me, God of my life,
for I feel weak and lack so much courage.
I place my trust in you.
Show me the way in which to terminate
this part of my experience.
Rescue me from the enemy of my past, God,
for in you I place my hope.
May your spirit guide me so that the coming days and
  years
of my journey will be ones in which I know
freedom, confidence and joy in the goodness of life.

After Ps 143:

   Write a brief letter of farewell to the person or situation or memory which you are ending. Pray for freedom. Pray for the one to whom you are writing the letter. (If praying for an event or an experience, pray for those involved.) Put the letter in your pocket. Open the closed door deliberately. Walk through it. Go outdoors, someplace where you can continue to be alone. Walk in the woods or the desert or along the beach or on the city streets. Find an appropriate place to be alone. Pray. Carefully, slowly tear the letter into small pieces as a sign of the break from the relationship. Place the pieces in a trash can or bury them in an appropriate place. Return to your room. Leave the door open as a sign of your new freedom and separation. Pray the scriptures.

Scripture

(Pray the entire psalm or passage suggested.)
Ps 146: The Lord sets captives free.
Ps 143: For the enemy pursues me.
2 Cor 4:7-18: Such an overwhelming power comes from God and not from us.

Closing prayer

God of beginnings and of endings, grant that I might have the strength to put an end to this matter which has weighed so heavily on my heart and my mind. Grant that I might bid farewell to this relationship which has brought me so much pain and grief. You know that this dying which is so evident in the process of termination will truly be a step into new life for me. I feel fragile and frail at this moment, even though I know it is the right direction and decision for me. Help me to close the door on this section of my journey, to walk into new rooms of life. I need to experience a freshness and a vitality like the cool breeze of a spring morning coming through an open window. Be this vitality for me, God of compassion. Grant that I may turn my back and walk away from what has been. I pray that I may be healed of this hurt and I pray that any whom I have hurt through this experience may also be healed. Amen.

Prayer When A Loved One Has Died

Image: a photo of the loved one

Take time to remember the special qualities which you so much loved and appreciated in your loved one's personality and life. Remember the special events in your lives that were full of joy and happiness. Offer thanks to God for all these blessings. Pour out your feelings of sadness and sorrow to God. Ask God to enter into the deep pain that permeates your life.

Prayer

"Father, I am coming to you!" (Jn 17:11).

Jesus, your departure was such an ache; your going away left a hollow in hearts, a tension between the love of your friends and the welcome awaiting you in going home to the Father. Such a mixture of feelings must have spun around in you: the sadness of your last farewell to friends and the anticipation of joy in the Father's welcome. You were leaving and sorely distressed. You were coming home and you were overjoyed.

Jesus, to the very end you lived our humanity, that life where one must always let go, must pass through death to enter into the fullness of life, that life where joy never completely buries sadness, where we move through days that demand goodbyes and come to moments that leave us no choice but to bid farewell to our loved ones.

Jesus, remind me in my own sad-heart time not to lose sight of the other side of ache, that glorious moment of happy homecoming, waiting for all of us in the loving hello of the Father. Send your Spirit to deepen my faith and to soften my sadness so that the vision of homecoming hopes will overpower the aches and struggles in all of life's farewells and goodbyes. Sustain me in this time of grief and comfort me as I experience this great loss in my life. Amen.

Scripture

Is 25:1-10 The Lord Yahweh will wipe away the tears from every cheek.

1 Thes 4:13-18 We believe that Jesus died and rose again; and that it will be the same for all those who have died in Jesus; God will bring them with him.

Reflection

Take some time in silence (or with gentle music) to listen to your feelings. What are the strongest feelings within your spirit? Be as honest as you can be with yourself. Remember that there are many aspects of grief and you may have feelings that you do not like or want such as self-pity, guilt, anger. . . . If you feel guilty, what has caused this in you? If you feel angry, what is there that is creating this feeling? After you have spent time surfacing your feelings, take each of your strongest ones and talk with God about them. Hold them out before God and ask God to take them from you.

Prayer

I take my loved one by the hand and lead her (him) to you, God of love. Here is _____ (name). Accept my love and thanksgiving as I entrust her (him) into your loving care. I want _____ to be free to be at home with you. I ask that you save a place for me there beside her (him) and that you be my loving presence in

all the lonely moments that await me. I ask that you fill
me with motivation and energy in the days ahead when
I feel like giving up; remind me often of my true homeland when I am caught up in the desolation of the journey. Help me to find joy in the people, events, and the
beauty of nature which surround me.

Thank you for the gift of _____ in my life. I want
to believe that we will celebrate the treasure of our love
again, when we are both in your presence forever. May
this truth sustain me in the days to come. Take my sad
and aching heart and comfort me. Comfort me, for I
can only feel hollowness and emptiness. God of the
sorrowing, draw near! Amen.

Prayer For Trust When Experiencing a Loss

Image: open hands

Prayer

God of mystery, I turn my heart to you. I come before
you in need of peace, grateful for the mystery of life
and ever keenly aware of your promises of guidance and
protection. I want to place my trust in you but my heart
grows fearful and anxious. I forget so easily that you
will be with me in all that I experience. Teach me to
be patient with the transformation of my life and to be
open to the change which I am now going through.

Reflection

Look at the geese of the sky: they neither worry nor
are anxious about the winter warnings of their life, for
they know within their deepest selves that their journey

will take them to a place of shelter, of comfort, of nourishment, a place where winter harshness cannot reach
them. See how they fly, winging homeward with sure-
ness, with trust in their hearts' instinct. If these geese,
who have not the faith and grace of human hearts, can
follow the mystery and secrets of their deepest selves,
cannot you, my loved and chosen ones, you whom I
care for as my very own, cannot you be in touch with
the mystery of your hearts? Cannot you trust in me to
guide you on your journey of life? For I have promised
to give you rest in seasons of tiredness, comfort in seasons of sorrow, peace in seasons of distress, strength in
seasons of great weakness. Trust in me. Do not be
afraid. I am with you. I will be your peace.

Scripture

> *"Peace I bequeath to you,*
> *my own peace I give you,*
> *a peace the world cannot give, this is my gift to you,*
> *Do not let your hearts be troubled or afraid"*
> *(Jn 14:27).*

After reading and reflecting on the scripture verse,
place your hands on your lap, palms up. Open them,
ready to give and to receive from God. Sit quietly for
several minutes in this posture of openness and trust.
Pray for the gift of trust in God as you go through this
experience of loss. Then read the following psalm
verses:

> *Yahweh is my strength, my shield,*
> *my heart puts its trust in God.*
> *I have been helped, my flesh has bloomed again;*
> *I thank God with all my heart (Ps 28:7).*

This I believe: I shall see the goodness of Yahweh
in the land of the living.
Put your hope in Yahweh, be strong; let your heart be
  bold,
put your hope in Yahweh (Ps 27:13-14).

I, for my part, like an olive tree
growing in the house of God,
put my trust in God's love
forever and ever (Ps 52:8).

My God, my God, why have you deserted me?
How far from saving me, the words I groan!
I call all day, my God, but you never answer,
all night long I call and cannot rest.
Yet, Holy One, you
who make your home in the praises of Israel,
in you our ancestors put their trust,
they trusted you and you rescued them;
they called to you for help and they were saved;
they never trusted you in vain (Ps 22:1-5).

Closing Prayer

God, in whom I trust, there is a part of me that is
dying and a part of me that is coming to life. I want to
have an open hands attitude toward you and toward my
life, but it is such a struggle to do so. Remind me often
of the peace which you extend to me. Thank you for
your beloved son who suffered and gave me an example
of trusting in you. Renew me day by day. Encourage
me so that I may always be faithful to your call deep
within my heart. I open myself to the mystery of life
and to your love. Amen.

Prayer of One Who Waits in Darkness

Image: darkness

Pray this prayer in darkness, either before dawn or after dusk. Find a room or a place where you can begin by just sitting in silence. As you sit, let the darkness you feel in your life be very present to you. After some time, light a candle or turn on a lamp.

Reflection

Suddenly there was a great burst of light through the Darkness. The light spread out and where it touched the Darkness, the Darkness disappeared. The light spread until the patch of Dark thing had vanished, and there was only a gentle shining, and through the shining came the stars, clear and pure. Then, slowly, the shining dwindled until it, too, was one, and there was nothing but stars and starlight. No shadows. No fear. Only the stars and the clear darkness of space, quite different from the fearful darkness of the Thing.

A Wrinkle in Time, Madeleine L'Engle.

Prayer: Ps 27 "Yahweh is my light and my salvation."

Scripture

Jn 1:1-5 A light that shines in the dark, a light that darkness could not overpower.

Ps 18: 28-32 My God lights up my darkness.

After reading the scripture passages, image yourself in darkness and then see God as the great light coming to light up all that is bleak and dark in you. Just rest in the goodness of that light.

During the coming days, be very aware of the natural and artificial light in your life. (For instance, when you switch on a light, headlights on the car, street lights, sunlight.) Each time, let this awareness be a quiet prayer within you to God who is your light. Trust God to shine in your darkness.

Prayer

God of light, hear my prayer. Listen to me and guide me in this deep darkness which is so predominant in my life. I feel as though an enemy is hounding me, trying to crush me. It presses against me until all of my world feels black and empty. You have been a source of light to me so many times in the past. I remember this with gratitude and I turn now to yearn for your light.

Here I am, hands outstretched. Oh, do not hide the radiance of inner light from me. I fear that I may be overpowered by discouragement or despair. May the dawn of each new day become a sign for me to trust in you. Help me to believe that your light is radiant within me. Light of my life, shine brightly and dispel this darkness. Amen.

Prayer of Goodbye to the Lies of My Life

Image: a transparent glass or a clear window pane

It is time to say goodbye to whatever is not truthful in your life. It may be a way of living, an attitude, a harsh judgment of yourself or others, an inner battle, thoughts or feelings that have kept you from being your true self or some resistance in you toward a person, an event, a situation.

Place the glass where you can see it or sit before a clear window pane. Invite God into your life. You may wish to use the following prayer:

God of truth, I come to you with a deep desire to be rid of all that keeps me from honesty, integrity, sincerity. I have allowed areas of my life to be ruled by non-truths. In these areas my spirit has been opaque, hid in delusions, unfree, clouded with deceit, unable to have you shine through. Make of me a transparent spirit, a person through whom truth radiates and integrity is clearly seen. I pray to have an inner world which reflects your goodness. As I sit here before this transparent object, I ask for the grace to let go of the untruths of my life. Lead me into freedom and into the strength which comes from living in truth and integrity.

Pause to reflect upon this quote:

"There is an inmost center in us where truth abides in fullness." (Mohandas Gandhi).

Reflection

Look at the glass or window pane. Notice its clearness, its transparency. Image a place in your heart where truth lives, where the gospel can clearly be seen in you. Go to this place and dwell there in silence for a while. Then go to a place in your heart where truth does not live, the place which is clouded, opaque. Reflect on this dimension of your inner life. Then write down your area(s) of dishonesty or deceit.

Scripture

Is 65:15-25 Whoever asks to be blessed on earth will ask to be blessed by the God of truth. . . .

Jn 8:31-32 "You will learn the truth, and the truth will make you free."

Prayer

> *"What do you want me to do for you?"*
> *"Sir . . . let me see again!"* (Lk 18:35-43).

Jesus, I too need to see again, to have that inner vision which bears the truth restored in me. Take me and transform me; shake loose all that has a hold on me and creates shutters on my inner eye, keeping out hopes, dreams and enthusiasm.

Awaken and stir up my heart in love; renew in me the desire to praise you; cast aside all my brokenness and throw off the dust of discouragement that layers my tired spirit.

Erase the glaze of mediocrity which hides the vision of the gospel. Draw me to your very own self where I can again be set on fire and filled with the wonder of discipleship.

Yes, Jesus, I want to see again, to know the direction to your doorstep. This will happen only if I allow you to do the touching, healing, the re-visioning of my inner life. Here I am, Lord, I come to do your will! Please, Lord, let me see again. My blindness needs your loving touch. Amen.

Listen to the Song: "Turn to Me," John Foley, S.J. (from the album *Earthen Vessels*)

Closing Prayer

Jesus, thank you for being so near, for walking with me as I struggle to come to terms with the lies of my life. You are the truth. I beg of you to keep placing in my spirit the yearning to be honest. I also pray that I can accept the fact that I shall always have some flaws and shadows in my heart, that the search for integrity shall always be a dimension of my life. Remind me often, at the core of who I am, that I am very good, that you love me as I am, while you long for me to be whole, honest and free. Amen.

Prayer of Parents Whose Child Has Died

Image: photos, mementos of the child who has died

> *Up, cry out in the night-time*
> *in the early hours of darkness;*
> *pour your heart out like water*
> *before Yahweh.*
> *Stretch out your hands to him*
> *for the lives of your children (Lam 2:19).*

Sit quietly and look at the mementos of your child. Remember all that you loved about this child. Let the grief and sorrow in you come forth. Let it spill out and be laid bare. Share with one another the memories you most cherish about your child.

Scripture

Read Lam 3:1-24.

This is a lament, a cry of great distress and mourning, by one who is overcome with grief. The Hebrew people were not afraid to cry out their pain and anger. It was a step toward healing and consolation.

After the reading, pause and reflect: What do you cry out to God? (You may wish to share this with one another.)

Litany of Grief

(One spouse or family member reads the statement. The other(s) responds.)
Response to each statement: God, be near to us, be our strength.

We remember our lives, the way they were before our child died. How we yearn for those moments when all was well, when we looked forward to future growth together. . . .

Every season will bring memories to us. Everywhere we turn we will recall the gift of our loved one. We will always remember the joys and the treasures of our dear one. . . .

There will forever be an empty spot in our lives because we have lost our child. He (she) can never be replaced. We search for inner peace and we strain for a sense of acceptance of this reality. . . .

Many feelings stir within us. We hurt with the heartache of our loss. Help us to believe that the sorrow will lessen as the days go on. . . .

Our relationship with one another is influenced by this death of our child. It may be hard to share the terrible ache, to enter into the other's sorrow. Help us to share this heavy burden of loss. May our marriage grow stronger, not weaker; may our love deepen, not lessen, as we go through this grief together. . . .

(If other children in family)
The children who live with us need our attention and

our love. May our grief over our child who has died not take away the love and affection which are so rightly theirs and which is so necessary for their own grieving time. . . .

We long for consolation and peace in our lives. We want to believe that our beloved child rests in the tender care of your loving arms, God. Deepen the belief in us that our child is home with you. . . .

Reflection

Read Jn 19:25-27; 38-42. Quietly image Mary standing beneath the cross. Then see her with her dead son in her arms. Reflect on what her feelings, her thoughts must have been. How did she feel as she left Jesus in the tomb? Put yourself in Mary's place. See yourself as Mary and your child as Jesus.

Mary, you held Jesus all through your life. It was an embrace begun in joy, cradling him in your womb's world, then as a vulnerable infant resting warm against your breast. You fearfully drew him close as you fled into a foreign land; you held him gratefully as you finally went home. You reached out and hugged him often all through those Nazareth years, binding up his childhood wounds and blessing his successes. You welcomed him in great relief as you found your lost one in the temple; you kissed him farewell as he went to his ministry and you rejoiced in all the good that he did. Mary, you held your child again on that terrible day of darkness, with his wounded, ragged body stripped helplessly before all. You received him as a parent, into your arms of desolation. He who had been so welcomed in your womb now had to be left behind in a darkened tomb. Mary, on that day you wept with all the parents of the world who had lost a child so fresh with life and so fragile with the reckoning of the human condition.

Closing Prayer (together)

God, we thank you for the gift of our _____
(name). You know what a treasure he (she) has been
for us. It is not easy to part with him (her). The days
are hard ones for us. The memories are there. Bless the
hurt in our hearts as we trudge along through each day.
Give us the energy we need to live our lives well. Do
not allow us to move into bitterness and alienation with
you or with one another. We can get through this painful time in our lives and we can go on with your strength
to sustain us. Grant us peace. Amen.

Prayer to Unite With Jesus in Suffering

Image: a cross

Make this cross out of two twigs or two small pieces
of wood. Tie the two pieces together with yarn or string.
Let the forming of this cross be an opening of your
spirit in uniting with the cross of Jesus.

Let us not lose sight of Jesus who leads us in our
faith and brings it to perfection: For the sake of the
joy which was still in the future he endured the cross
(Heb 12:2).

During his life on earth, he (Jesus) offered up prayer
and entreaty, aloud and in silent tears (Heb 5:1-10).

Prayer

Jesus, Suffering One, you know how overwhelmed I am
with the pain in my life. You, too, hurt in so many
ways. Inner pain took you over at times. You wept salty
tears of sadness over Jerusalem and for your friend,
Lazarus. You must have wept within your heart, too, as
you struggled for truth to happen in a broken world.
You offered prayer. You questioned. You pleaded.

I want to walk with you, to learn from you. I desire to
give you my love in total and complete surrender and
fidelity. I feel as though this deep hurt will overpower
me, that I shall be overcome by it. There is a deep
canyon of desolation in me.

Be my strength so that I will not give up. Be my vision
so that I can see how to live through this suffering. Be
my companion of love and guide me each moment of
every day.

Scripture

> I believe that nothing can happen that will outweigh
> the supreme advantage of knowing Christ Jesus my
> Lord. For him I have accepted the loss of every-
> thing. . . . All I want is to know Christ and the pow-
> er of his resurrection and to share his sufferings by
> reproducing the pattern of his death (Phil 3:7-8,10).

When we are feeling overwhelmed by suffering, it is
helpful to go and sit by the cross of Jesus, to hear his
cry, to see his pain, to know that he understands and
sees ours.

Sit quietly. Hold the cross you have made in your
hands. Reflect on one dimension of the passion that
most relates to your own particular suffering:

- Sit with him in love at the table of the bread where he experiences the sadness of farewell (Lk 22:14-20).
- Kneel with him in the garden agony where he struggles with surrender (Lk 22:39-46).
- Walk with him to the place of his betrayal (Mt 26:47-56).
- Hear the jeers and insults flung at him in derision (Lk 22:63-65).
- Stand with his mother bent in sorrow (Jn 19:25-27).
- Cry out with him in surrender to the Father (Lk 23:44-46).
- Bathe his wounds and gently lay him in the tomb (Jn 19:38-42).
- Sojourn with the faithful ones who mourn his going (Mt 27:61).

After this reflection, review your own sufferings. Name them. Place them on the cross you have made. (Either do this with mental imagery or by writing them on paper and placing them on the cross.) Keep the cross in a room where you can often see it so that you may draw strength from the memory of your prayer.

Closing Prayer (adapted from 2 Cor 4:5-12)

God of hope, I unite with your son, Jesus, and I renew my belief in your loving power and strength. I believe that even though I am in difficulties on all sides that I shall never be hopelessly cornered. Even though I see no answer to my problems, I need not despair. I may feel as though I am persecuted, but I will never be deserted by you. I may be knocked down, but never destroyed. Always, wherever I may be, I can draw strength and courage from the life, death and resurrection of Jesus. I will have my own time of transformation. I open myself to your light shining in my darkness and I rejoice in the overwhelming fidelity of your love in my life. Amen.

Prayer of One Who Feels Terribly Poor Inside

Image: anything empty (an empty cup, an empty seed pod, an empty box). Ponder the object before you. What does it say about your own emptiness?

Prayer

I do not feel that I have anything to offer to you, God, or to anyone else as far as that goes. Inside of me all is emptiness. I can only hear the echo of sadness. I am sitting in the ashes of desolation. I feel swallowed in a sea of nothingness. Come, let me know the strong refrains of your love running through my inner pockets of poverty. At these times, when I feel so alone, so powerless, so sad and so desolate, the promise of your love does not enthuse me or enhearten me. Take this empty spirit of mine, fill it with a deep belief in your abiding presence; allow me to bid farewell to whatever keeps me from relying on you. Help me to see that this emptiness can be a blessing because it puts my life in perspective and allows me to see you as the source of all inner energy and fullness. God of the poor, draw near to me in my need.

Scripture

1 Kgs 17:7-16 I have . . . only a handful of meal and
a little oil in a jug.

Phil 2:5-11 He (Jesus) did not cling to his equality
with God but emptied himself.

2 Cor 8:9 He became poor for your sake.

Reflection

''Poor in Spirit''

What is this tiny whisper in me?
it weaves a voice of hope
through the poorness of my heart,
sifting, sorting, searching,
always finding many things
to call forth its cry: Thank you!

This tiny whisper in me
is the silent breath of faith,
stirred by a God, intimately near,
a God who has eyes, unlike mine,
who can see in the deepest corners
of pain, anguish, question, doubt;
who can recognize in all of this
elements of growth and goodness.

God of all the stirrings in my heart,
see here, in this heart that is so poor,
the words of thanks formed in faith:
Thank you for all those life events
that I've fought and struggled with.

Thank you for all those surrenders
that seared and pained and burned;

thank you for the restlessness
that loomed up large against my soul.

Thank you for all that appeared to be empty,
for without those parts of my life
I would not be so poor in spirit,
nor nearly so ready to turn to you.

Closing Prayer

God of the wandering ones, God of those who have so little, from the chasm of my emptiness I draw out the meagerness of my prayer and I come to you. Everything is dry and fruitless inside me. All the richness of past consolations has disappeared. I feel void of even your presence and love. This time of experiencing my poorness is purifying and sometimes very discouraging. Your word teaches that the poor in spirit are blessed, that these empty ones will inherit the kingdom of heaven (Mt 5:3). Is this poorness in my heart a part of that truth? Are you calling me to a deeper and fuller reliance upon you alone? Are you allowing me to be challenged in my spiritual journey so that I will choose where my treasure is, so that I will make more room for you in my heart? I still fight the empty days and nights; I still search for a prayer life that feels good; I still want to be perfect instead of loving myself with my flaws as well as my strengths. Will you teach me how to live with my inner poorness? Will you enable me to let go of clutching and grasping after fullness? Draw me to your heart and bless me, your poor and needy servant. Amen.

Prayer for One Going to a New Ministry

Image: a bowl of fruit and some seeds

Begin by reading and praying these scripture passages: Gen 12:1-19; Ex 6:2-13.

Reflect on:

- the call of God in your life
- the love relationship that you have with God and the people of God
- your own Egypt (Is there anything in you that enslaves and keeps you from being free to move on?)
- the covenant and the promises of God
- the blessings of your past days and years of ministry
- the hopes you have for the future

Hold the bowl of fruit in your hands. Raise it in gratitude to God for all of your blessings.

Hold the seeds in your hands. Raise them in intercession for the dreams and goals of your new ministry.

Reflection "The Sowing and the Going"

> *"I did the planting, Apollos did the watering,*
> *but God made things grow. Neither the planter*
> *nor the waterer matters; only God, who makes*
> *things grow." (1 Cor 3:6-7).*

> *Days of hard hoeing*
> *careful setting of seeds,*
> *delight of daylight,*
> *announcement of green touches.*
> *Earthened secrets give birth.*

After hours in the garden,
a greater meaning comes
between the tiny radishes
and tender shoots of asparagus.

Autumn will find me elsewhere,
the garden left to harvest
by hands that never knew
the birth of its greening.

So, too, with my ministry.
The garden encircles the truth:
Sowing and going are trademarks,
familiar patterns, for disciples.

The tug of the sowing and going
is tempered by the stronger hold
of a much greater Gardener,
one who sowed first face of seed,
who entrusted the growth to others,
and gave himself to the going.

Thus it is that I stand reflectively
in a garden so much smaller,
praying the heart of sowing and going,
and wanting to join in the journey.

Closing Prayer

"You will leave with joy and be led away in safety."
(Is 55:12).

Yahweh, God of the journey, you went with the Israelites in the form of a pillar of cloud by day to show them the way and by night in the form of a pillar of fire to give them light for their journey (Ex 13:21-22). I long for that kind of assuredness of your presence on my new road, too. I fear the unknown and I wonder what the future will hold for me. A part of me wants to hold

onto the blessings I have known and to rest in the security that is mine.

Remind me often that I am to bring the good news,
that I am your servant, a herald of justice and peace
(Is 52:7). May I be so open to your word and your way
as I travel on that people will "take me by the sleeve"
and say: "We want to go with you since we have learnt
that God is with you." (Zec 8:23). Encourage me with
a deepened awareness of my calling when I want to
look back or when I experience feelings of loneliness,
doubt or homelessness. Take me to your people and
shine through my life. Amen.

Prayer to Accept a Parent

Image: anything flawed or imperfect (for example, a plate
with a crack or a chip on it, a paper with a torn edge, a
pencil without an eraser, something partly worn out)

Ponder

Begin by looking at the flawed object you have chosen. Reflect on your grievances toward your parent.
How have you been hurt? What flaws or weaknesses in
this parent have you found difficult or harmful? List
these. When the list is complete, trace a cross over what
you have written. Let the cross signify the pain that has
been yours as you have struggled with this parent.

Prayer

God, you have shown yourself as a welcoming father
(Lk 15:11-32) and a tender mother (Lk 13:34-35). I have

yearned to have my own parent be like you. I feel wounded, disappointed in the behavior that I have experienced. There is constant struggle and pain in this relationship. Deep down inside I yearn to have him (her) meet my needs and expectations for love and acceptance. It is difficult to love my father (mother) because of the human weaknesses and flaws which I so easily see. I have a mixture of feelings tumbling in me—anger, guilt, discouragement, love, self-doubts, concern.

You are a God who heals the wounded. You bless the pain in us when we are overcome with the hurts of life. You promise us a future full of hope (Jer 29). See here in my spirit all the hurt of the past. Heal me of my disillusionment, the distress of differences, the heartaches and tensions over past problems. I beg of you to help me to forgive my parent for his (her) faults. I also beg assistance in lowering my expectations of all I want my parent to be for me. Help me to see the strengths and the goodness which are also there. Most of all, draw me to a deep love which accepts this parent as he (she) is.

Ponder

Reflect once more on your parent. Image yourself within the womb, a tiny person being given life and personality. Pause in gratitude for the life which has been given to you by your parents. Then reflect on the good qualities and characteristics of this parent. When completed, draw a heart over these words to signify the blessings this parent has shared with you or with others.

Scripture

1 Cor 13:1-13
Lk 6:36-38

Pray for the gifts of compassion, understanding, kindness, mercy. Pray to forgive your parent for the wrongs which have been knowingly or unknowingly done to you. Image God receiving love from you and placing it in the heart of your parent. Image God receiving love from your parent and placing it in your heart.

Closing Prayer

Long ago I was being formed in the womb. I was becoming. The gracious gift of life took hold in me and I burst forth into myself. The first gift given to me by my parent was this wonderful blessing of vitality. I am grateful.

Forgiving and understanding God, you see into my heart and you understand. You know the struggles which have been mine and you are aware of the clashes that are so much a part of the relationship which I have with this parent. It is time for me to move on from all of this. It is time for me to let go of trying to change my parent or make him (her) into someone who would be all I want him (her) to be. I can only let go of this with your power and strength working through me, enabling me to be myself while allowing my father (mother) to be his (her) self, too.

Encircle my being with patience and kindness so that I will not give up trying to offer this acceptance and unconditional love. Help me to overlook the faults and to focus on the good qualities which are also there.

Bless my parent in his (her) aging. May I be a support as his (her) health fails. Let me not hold his (her) weaknesses against him (her) or hold back the love of my heart. Finally, God, may I learn how to accept the parent that I have and let go of the parent I hoped to have. Amen.

Prayer of One Weary With Walking Others Through Their Goodbyes

Image: Simon carrying the cross for Jesus

Reflection

"Called to Be Simon"

"As they were leading him away they seized on a man, Simon from Cyrene, who was coming in from the country, and made him shoulder the cross and carry it behind Jesus." (Lk 23:26).

I've never thought of myself as Simon the cross-carrier;
Life is not at all the way I had it planned.
I stand beside a broken spirit, another human in need.
I listen. I empathize. I hear. I resist.
I know without a doubt what is being asked of me:
I am called to be Simon to that struggling Christ in her;
unable to bear the weight alone, she needs support, love.
I want to run away, not carry. It costs too much.
It's too demanding and much too heavy to bear.

Carrying others' crosses, bearing others' burdens,
it's wearing and so very time consuming.
(Jesus, can't you find someone else?
I'd rather choose my own wood to wear.)

Yet, Lord, there you look at me:
the same sorrow that I see in her eyes,

the same weight of spirit that she bears,
the same weakness of which she cries out.
I've never thought of myself as Simon walking with you.
Yet, here I am before you, struggling with the journey.
It's not what I'd have chosen. I fight against it even now,
but there the cross is, waiting to be worn.
If only I hold out my arms. If only I open my heart.

Meditation

Take the suffering Jesus with you to someone else in your life who suffers, someone whose life has been entwined with yours and to whom you have been Simon. See Jesus reach out and touch that person with deep peace and love.

Bring your own weariness of walking with this person who suffers. See yourself as Simon of Cyrene. Hold out to God the hurts and distress, the negative feelings which you may have because you carry another's cross or walk with another in his or her sorrows. Ask God to renew your love and your strength.

Scripture

Mt 11:28-30   ''Come to me, all you who are . . . over-
               burdened.''
Gal 6:2   You should carry each others' troubles.
Is 40:29-31   God gives strength to the wearied.

Song for listening: "Come to Me All Who Are Weary," Dan Schutte, S.J. (album: *Neither Silver Nor Gold*)

Closing Prayer

Mary, beloved in the heart of a God-made-flesh,
you were asked to faithfully carry Christ-wombed,

to bravely be with him in darkest death-suffering,
receiving his agony in the arms of your compassion.

Mary, I am the beloved of this same God,
carrying the Christ in my own heart's womb,
reaching out to receive another who hurts and aches,
embracing one in the turmoil of transformation.

Mary, teach me through your vulnerable stance
to embrace those who are wounded and wrapped in pain;
draw me to touch reverently the raw-edge hurts,
the hollow places in people's aching lives,
to be there as tenderly, as faithfully as you were.

Teach me how to stand near to the cross,
help me to see that the fragments of death
are gathered in time into a loving wholeness,
healed by a God who loved the world so much
that an only Son was sent to suffer with it.

Prayer of One Who Needs Inner Healing

Image: a Band-Aid

Spend some time identifying what needs to be healed in you. (What is your hurt, your wound, your pain?)

Read Ez 34:11-16
Pause to let the words of verse 16 rest in your soul:

"I shall look for the lost one, bring back the stray, bandage the wounded and make the weak strong."

Prayer

God of love, you are the shepherd and I am one of your flock. The words of Ezechiel speak to me of your comforting presence and the truth of your care. I bear so much hurt inside from what has happened to me. My inner world has been one of anxiety and distress. In Ezechiel you promise never to let me out of your sight, to look after me and to keep me from harm. You assure me that you will rescue me when I am scattered, that you will draw me close when I lose my way in the mist and the darkness created by my wounds.

The pain of my hurts keeps me in a foreign land where I do not feel at home with myself or others. Help me to believe that you will lead me into a future rich with growth and peace. Show me where to rest, how to lay down my burdens and what to do in order to be healed.

Loving shepherd, I need to find a source of new life. Come, bandage my wounds and grant to this weak one a profound and deep strength to go on. Amen.

Scripture

Is 57: 18-19 "I will indeed heal."
Is 35:1-10 The scorched earth becomes a lake,
the parched land springs of water.
Is 58:6-11 "Your wound will quickly be healed over."

After reading and meditating on the scripture carefully remove the Band-Aid as a sign of your faith in God's healing power.

Closing Prayer

Jesus, you cured those who were in need of healing (Lk 9:11). Take me by the hand as you did so many on your journeys, and help me to rise up. I need to walk with a renewed strength and vigor. Stretch out your hand and touch all within me that needs to be healed.

The power which goes out from you can penetrate my being and cure what ails my spirit.

To the blindness in me you say: "Shed the darkness. Look! See!" To whatever is withered, bent, crippled within me, you proclaim: "Be freed! Go and walk your best in the world." To the hunger in me for truth, beauty, peace, consolation, you promise: "I will feed you." To my distressed, disconnected, confused dimensions you say: "I will bring you to your senses." To the deaf and the unlistening parts of my heart you speak: "Be opened!" To all that has died in me and needs to rise up, you call out: "Come forth!"

I need your touch. I need your words. Jesus, healer, draw me to yourself. Amen.

Prayer of One Who Yearns for a New Heart

Image: dry bones

Read Ez 37:1-14

Image yourself as the dry bones. Feel the deadness, emptiness, void, or brokenness in your heart rise and grow into new life. See the bones coming together to form a person—you—alive, energized, renewed.

Prayer

Spirit of God, I feel too tired to go on, too empty even to want to be filled, too broken to put the pieces together again. Still, I feel a quiet stirring in me. It is the call to come back to life, to be energized and renewed. It is my heart crying out for newness, for a lighter spirit, for a keener sense of hope in the future.

Spirit of God, who draws together bones of the desert

and dryness of the heart, come and take of my spirit all
that has died in me. Dream in me again. Create of my
brokenness a new and free heart. Draw together life in
me. Let the dancing that's meant to be start its movement anew. The grace of freedom, the gesture of re-
birth, all of this awaits me. I want to believe it in my
depths.

Reflection

Listen to some of your favorite music. Let it fill your
being with hope, with a sense of new life. Or, if you
have a green plant, take the plant and touch the leaves.
See the new life in it. Ponder the energy and vitality
that flows through the plant.

Scripture

Ez 36:24-26   "I shall give you a new heart, and put a
                new spirit in you."
Is 43:18-21   "See, I am doing a new deed."

Closing Prayer

> *A clean heart create in me, O God,*
> *and a steadfast spirit renew within me (Ps 51).*

These words come on the wings of the morning. They
are your quiet yet urgent messengers to me. For I do,
indeed, need a clean heart, God. I need a heart that is
free from the dross of the past, a heart that is fresh with
enthusiasm and energy for the present as well as for the
future. A steadfast heart is what I want to claim, a heart
that does not waver about the truth or fall short when
it comes to loving well. Do not allow the events of the

past to dominate my memory or chain my heart to negative feelings. Move me beyond this, God of new hearts. Fill my entire being with a fresh freedom so that I will walk the journey as well as possible. Create in me a vibrant spirit, one that carries hope, one that believes in peace. Take this heart of mine and fill it with your goodness. Amen.

Selected Bibliography

Anderson, Herbert, and Kenneth Mitchell. *All Our Losses, All Our Griefs* (Philadelphia: Westminster Press, 1983).

Augsburger, David. *When Enough Is Enough:* Discovering True Hope When All Hope Seems Lost (Ventura, CA.: Regal Books, 1984).

Bloomfield, Harold H. with Leonard Felder. *Making Peace With Your Parents* (New York: Ballantine Books, 1985).

Bozarth-Campbell, Alla. *Life Is Goodbye, Life Is Hello:* Grieving Through All Kinds of Loss (Minneapolis: CompCare, 1982).

Brennan, Anne, and Brewi, Janice. *Midlife Directions* (New York: Paulist Press, 1985).

Bridges, William. *Transitions:* Making Sense of Life's Changes (Menlo Park, CA: Addison-Wesley Publishing Co., 1980).

Colgrove, Bloomfield, McWilliams. *How to Survive the Loss of a Love* (Toronto: Bantam Books, 1976).

Eliade, Mircea. *Images and Symbols* (New York: Sheed and Ward, 1961).

Fenocketti, Mary M. *Coping With Pain* (Liguori, MO: Liguori, 1982).

Fisher, Kathleen R. *The Inner Rainbow: The Imagination in Christian Life* (New York: Paulist Press, 1983).

Fox, Matthew. *Original Blessings:* A Primer in Creation Spirituality. (Sante Fe, NM: Bear and Co., 1983).

Frankl, Viktor. *Man's Search for Meaning* (New York: Washington Square Press, 1963).

Grollman, Earl A. *Living When a Loved One Has Died* (Boston: Beacon Press, 1977).

Hays, Edward. *Pray All Ways* (Easton, KS: Forest of Peace Books, 1981).

Heagle, John. *Our Journey Toward God* (Chicago: Thomas More Press, 1977).

John Paul II. "The Christian Meaning of Human Suffering" (*Origins*, Vol. 13, No. 37, February 23, 1974).

Kubler-Ross, Elisabeth. *Death, the Final Stage of Life* (Englewood Cliffs, NJ: Prentice Hall, 1973).

Kubler-Ross, Elisabeth. *On Death and Dying* (New York: Macmillan, 1969).

Kushner, Harold. *When Bad Things Happen to Good People* (New York: Avon Books, 1981).

Lewis, C.S. *A Grief Observed* (New York: Seabury Press, 1963).

Lewis, C.S. *The Problem of Pain* (New York: Macmillan, 1962).

Linn, Matthew, Linn, Dennis, Fabricant, Sheila. *Prayer Course for Healing Life's Hurts* (New York: Paulist Press, 1983).

Marty, Martin E. *A Cry of Absence: Reflections for the Winter of the Heart* (San Francisco: Harper & Row, 1983).

Moustakas, Clark E. *Loneliness* (Englewood Cliffs, NJ: Prentice Hall, 1961).

Nouwen, Henri. *In Memoriam* (Notre Dame: Ave Maria Press, 1980).

Raines, Robert A. *Going Home:* A Personal Story of Self Discovery, A Journey from Despair to Hope (San Francisco: Harper & Row, 1979).

Sheehy, Gail. *Pathfinders* (New York: Bantam Books, 1982).

Smedes, Lewis B. *How Can It Be All Right When Everything Is All Wrong?* (San Francisco: Harper & Row, 1982).

Soelle, Dorothee. *Suffering* (Philadelphia: Fortress Press, 1975).

Stein, Murray. *In Mid-Life* (Dallas, TX: Spring Publications, 1983).

Stearns, Ann Kaiser. *Living Through Personal Crisis* (Chicago: The Thomas More Press, 1984).

Sullender, R. Scott. *Pastoral Resources for Emotional and Spiritual Growth* (New York: Paulist Press, 1985).

Tagore, Rabindranath, *Gitanjali:* A Collection of Indian Songs (New York: Macmillan, 1971).

Wiederkehr, Macrina, O.S.B. *Seasons of Your Heart* (New Jersey: Silver Burdette, 1979).

Westberg, Granger E. *Good Grief* (Philadelphia: Fortress Press, 1962, 1971).

Westermann, Claus. *Praise and Lament in the Psalms* (Atlanta, GA: John Knox Press, 1981).

Whitehead, Evelyn and James. *Christian Life Patterns* (New York: Doubleday, 1979).

Whitehead, Evelyn Eaton and James D. *Seasons of Strength* (New York: Doubleday, 1986).

About the Author

Sister Joyce Rupp, osm, is active in retreat programs, lay ministry enrichment, and religious formation. This book emerges from her experience in teaching a course on goodbyes and the grieving process. Her previous book, *Fresh Bread and Other Gifts of Spiritual Nourishment*, as well as numerous magazine articles, establishes her reputation as a gifted spiritual writer. A member of the Servite community, she holds a master's degree in religious education and participates in ongoing studies in spirituality and theology at Creighton University and the University of Notre Dame. She is currently resource theologian for the St. Joseph's Educational Center in Des Moines.